Frederick Charles Woodhouse

A Manual For Advent

A few thoughts for every day, and for Christmastide and the New Year

Frederick Charles Woodhouse

A Manual For Advent

A few thoughts for every day, and for Christmastide and the New Year

ISBN/EAN: 9783741192180

Manufactured in Europe, USA, Canada, Australia, Japa

Cover: Foto ©Lupo / pixelio.de

Manufactured and distributed by brebook publishing software (www.brebook.com)

Frederick Charles Woodhouse

A Manual For Advent

A MANUAL FOR ADVENT.

A MANUAL FOR ADVENT:

A Few Thoughts for Every Day,

AND FOR

Christmastide and the New Year.

BY

F. C. WOODHOUSE, M.A.

AUTHOR OF
"A MANUAL FOR LENT," "THE LIFE OF THE SOUL IN THE WORLD,"
ETC. ETC.

"Behold, I come quickly.
Even so, come, Lord Jesus."

Second Edition.

LONDON:
WELLS GARDNER, DARTON, & CO.
2 PATERNOSTER BUILDINGS.

PREFACE.

EACH Christian Season, as it comes round, seems to be the most important. That portion of the Catholic faith which it specially brings before us, appears for the time to occupy the whole horizon, and to leave no room for anything else.

What, for instance, can be more momentous to the man conscious of his responsibility and his immortality, than the great truth of Judgment to come, which the Church bids us ponder upon and realise during Advent? What can be so important to any one as that he should die a good death? What better antidote to the seductions of temptation; what more powerful stimulus to the right use of time; what can sober pride or keep down ambition more surely than the conviction that death is approaching, the end of this life, the beginning of the life eternal that will take its shape from the deeds, words, and thoughts of these passing years? "Remember the end, and thou shalt never do amiss."

Or again, what truth is so blessed as the Christian revelation of "God manifest in the flesh," a Saviour born for sinners? Does it not seem as if we wanted nothing else? Do we not fancy that as

> "A little helpless innocent bird,
> That has but one plain passage of few notes,
> Will sing the simple passage o'er and o'er
> For all an April morning;"

so we could be content to take for our life-theme, "Unto you is born a Saviour"?

But the thought of Death, if constantly dwelt upon, would make us morbid, and an undue and excessive fear of the terrors of Judgment has made men frantic or desperate. So with any other article of our Creed, any other Gospel truth, it may be abused and made positively mischievous if it be allowed to engross the whole attention, and if other equally important portions of the Faith be forgotten or disparaged.

It is only by the admirable economy of the Church's system that "the proportion of faith" is preserved. No dogma can exclusively or disproportionately occupy the minds of those who dutifully follow the Church's guidance; and none can be forgotten. For when we have been occupied with one long enough, we are obliged to pass on to some other great truth, which the cycle of the Church's teaching brings before us.

Almost all error arises from excessive attachment to

some particular doctrine, to the exclusion of others. A truth may be perverted into heresy through the neglect of another truth which balances it. Just as madness, or eccentricity, or some failing that spoils a fine character, or ruins what might have been a useful and noble life, often arises from the abnormal and monstrous development of a faculty, or the dwarfing of a needful safeguard, so fanaticism, sectarianism, and half the mischief that well-meaning men have inflicted upon the world under the plea of religion, and zeal for God and for truth, have had their origin in ignorance of "the proportion of faith."

But let us take each wondrous thought as it comes, give ourselves up to it for its appointed Season, and then lay it aside, and bend our minds to the next, and all will be well. Thus, before we have been perverted, or soured, or crazed by meditation upon Death and Judgment, Heaven and Hell, we are summoned to Bethlehem to worship our Infant Saviour, and then presently we are raised from our knees, because a New Year has come, and we must be up and doing, making a new and better beginning of every duty. We remember that if Death is coming, Life is present; that if our Lord was once a little Child, He will some day sit as our Judge.

"Whatsoever thy hand findeth to do, do it with thy might." Just as the stately oak gains its massive solidity, its wide spread of branches—alone among trees defying gravitation by their horizontal expanse—by long successions of seasons, Springs, Summers, Autumns, Winters, sunshine and rain, cold and heat, wind and calm, again and again repeated, so let us throw ourselves unreservedly into the mind and spirit of the Church as each Season comes, and we shall be guided into all truth, and grow up and be established in the Faith, exaggerating nothing, neglecting nothing, blessed by each, made perfect by all.

CONTENTS.

	PAGE
Advent Sunday.—The Blessedness of Advent	1
Monday.—Responsibility	7
Tuesday.—Waiting for Christ	13
Wednesday.—Opposition to Custom	20
Thursday.—The Annihilation of Sin	28
Friday.—Balaam's Prayer	34
Saturday.—Who will be our Judge?	40
Second Sunday in Advent.—Perplexity	50
Monday.—Sins of Omission	58
Tuesday.—The Method of God's Judgment	63
Wednesday.—Blessed Purity	72
Thursday.—The Touch of Christ	79
Friday.—The Wickedness of the Unloving Heart	85
Saturday.—Christ's Brother, Sister, and Mother	91
Third Sunday in Advent.—The Mission of the Baptist Perpetual	101
Monday.—The Coming of Christ's Kingdom	107
Tuesday.—Christ's Kingdom within us	112

CONTENTS.

	PAGE
Wednesday.—What is our Own	118
Thursday.—The Dead Rule the World	126
Friday.—The Love of God Regenerate Man's Instinct	133
Saturday.—The Heroism of the Service of God . . .	138
Fourth Sunday in Advent.—Joy because of Christ's Coming	147
Monday.—Pharaoh's Butler and Baker Advent Types .	152
Tuesday.—Evil	160
St. Thomas.—The Advent Lessons of St. Thomas's Day .	168
Thursday.—The Reward of Work for God	173
Friday.—Praying for the Coming of Christ	179
Christmas Eve.—Going to Bethlehem	184
Christmas Day.—Jesus our Brother	189
St. Stephen.—The Two Great Mothers	195
St. John.—Meeting the Judge at Bethlehem . . .	200
Holy Innocents.—The Dominion of the Little Child . .	207
Thursday.—The Sign to the Shepherds and to the World .	213
Friday.—No Room for God	218
New Year's Eve.—The End of the World	224
New Year's Day.—Christ's First Taste of Human Sorrow .	234

Advent Sunday.

THE BLESSEDNESS OF ADVENT.

THE season of Advent has a twofold lesson for us all. We look back, and we look forward—back at the first great act of redemption, forward to the last and crowning event that shall set the unalterable seal of eternity upon our personal salvation. So we say, "Blessed is He that cometh in the name of the Lord;" blessed is the Babe of Bethlehem, the Author of our salvation; blessed is the glorious Lord God, coming in the clouds of heaven to restore all things, to abolish evil, to clothe us with purity and salvation, to bring us into the blessed presence of the good God. The Church "brings forth out of her treasures things new and old"—things old, very old, yet more precious because of their age, like the old wine ripened and mellowed with age. The old tale of man's redemption, the old tale of the hymning angels and the startled, listening, and rejoicing shepherds, the old sweet tale of the Virgin Mother and the wondrous Babe, of the wise men from the far East and their guiding star. It is an old tale; we have known it, thank God! as long as we have known anything, and we are not weary of it yet—no, nor ever shall be; it grows dearer to us every year, as we grow older, as we understand it better, and learn it more and more by heart.

But it is an older tale even than this. It is as old as the world. As soon as sin clouded the brightness of man's present, his eyes turned hither where the promise of the woman's Seed made a bright spot of hope in the future. When Eve's first-born came she thought it was her Redeemer; she thought she had gotten "the man from the Lord." When Noah was born men had still the same hope. Abraham, David, all the faithful in all ages, all mankind, with more or less clearness, have longed and yearned for the coming promised Saviour; all hearts and lips were tuned ready to sing the joyous song, "Blessed is He that cometh in the name of the Lord."

But the Advent season tells also of things new, things quite new, quite unknown, wonderful and strange beyond all experience, all imagination. We are told of the end of all things, of the bursting forth of the millions of the dead from beneath our feet and from the depths of the sea, the newly dead of yesterday, and the unknown dead of past ages and forgotten races; of the rending away for ever of the veil that hides spiritual things from us; of the sight of the angels that hover in their myriad hosts about us; of the sight of our own naked souls and of the souls of others, just as we are and have made ourselves in this daily life of probation; of the sight of God; of the sight of Christ in His glorified human flesh. We are told of judgment according to works; of life eternal, life new yet the same; of duration without time; of existence without decay. These are some of the things new and old which the Church brings forth for us out of her treasures at Advent-tide. These things she bids us gaze upon, think of, realise. For this she bids us separate ourselves more from the world, its duties and pleasures; for this she opens her churches more frequently; for this she sends us to our knees; upon this she bids us ponder and meditate, till we can say with faith and hope and gratitude, "Blessed is He that cometh in the name of the Lord."

The loving child listens for his father's step; the devoted wife yearns with empty heart for her absent husband; the poor prisoner counts the days that will bring him release; the sick man pines for the coming sweet rest of painless health; the aching labourer watches the shadow of the sinking sun; the wearied traveller exults at the sight of the spires of the long-desired city; the mother, with outstretched hand and eager hungry face and glistening eye and attentive ear, welcomes the friend that comes to tell her of her son, whom he has lately seen, and who is even now on his way home after long years of far-off wanderings. What preparations are there with all these for the desired meeting; how much is there to be done; what thought, what plans, what eagerness; how much in earnest they all are! This is the master idea, all else is made secondary, all must give place and wait for this.

Like all this then is Advent-tide to the faithful Christian. The Church's voice calls up such thoughts, such preparations. The Christian sinks upon his knees as he hears her message, his pulse quickens, his heart is agitated between fear and hope, till hope prevails, and the response of his lips comes spontaneously, "Blessed is He that cometh in the name of the Lord."

Let us for a moment look into his heart, the fountain-head of these words, and see whence and how they arise, why he so speaks and so feels at Advent-tide. It is something on this wise. The first thought is the human shrinking thought of terror, that old, old thought that first sprang up in man's heart when, after his defilement by sin, he heard the voice of God walking in the garden in the cool of the day, and drawing near to him, and calling him by name: "Depart from me, for I am a sinful man, O Lord; not yet; oh, not yet." Just as the loved one would not be surprised by its lover in unpreparedness, but would with all care look its best, and till then shrink silently away, so the soul that knows what God is, and what sin is, and what is its own sinfulness, cowers back from the approach of God, now deeply reddened with the blush of shame, now white with the agonies of fear. "If thou, Lord, art extreme to mark what is done amiss, O Lord, who may abide it?" And then, while yet there is time, there is the seeking of cleansing: "Wash me more and more from my iniquity, and cleanse me from my sin." The Bridegroom comes, the wedding-garment is put on, the lamp is trimmed. The Advent cry resounds, "The Bridegroom cometh," and the Christian soul betakes itself yet more earnestly to penitence; it cannot venture to meet God otherwise than at the foot of the Cross. Once more all the past life is examined, lest some secret sin should have escaped the searchings of confession, the healing, absolving applications of the Precious Blood. Once more the heart renounces all lords but the One long ago chosen; once more the breast is smitten, and the cry bursts forth, "Lord, I am not worthy!"

But the Christian soul cannot rest here. In the very midst of fear and penitence, another word forces its way, full of trust and love, "My Lord and my God; this is my Lord, I have waited for Him. Whom have I but Thee? there is none that I desire but Thee. Lord, Thou knowest that I love Thee." And then there crowd up a host of thoughts in long-hurrying succession; the thought of seeing God, the one Good, the one Beautiful, the one True; of seeing Jesus, Saviour, Friend, dear Master and Lord; the thought of freedom from sin and temptation, and danger of falling; the realising of yearning longings for purity; the fruition of the bliss of perfect love; the meeting of all loving pure souls, known and unknown; loving and being loved by all; the clearing up of all hard questions; the end of all painful endurance and suspense; the righting of all wrongs which loving hearts have groaned over, and loving hands have laboured to remove in vain—always, alas! in vain; the end of the contradiction of sinners, by which God is provoked every day; the explanation of all religious difficulties, and doubts, and controversies; the sweeping away for ever of all the miseries of this sinful world; the sheltering of the weak, the vindication of the slandered, the enriching of the poor, the rest of the weary, the speechless joy of the hopeless, the eternal banishment of evil, the eternal reign of good.

Thus and thus, and much more than words can utter, thinks the Christian man at the foot of the Cross at Advent-tide; and as he thinks his heart burns, his spirit is lifted up to meet the Lord, and his voice joins with all redeemed souls that wait for His appearing, and with the chorus of the blessed angels who rejoice in the joy of others: "Blessed is He that cometh in the name of the Lord; Hosanna in the highest."

Here let us stop. There are indeed other Advent thoughts; the coming of the Lord and the end of this world as it is brings other thoughts than these to some. The Church associates with this season the awful thought of judgment and condemnation, and that, the most awful thought that the human mind can grasp, the thought of lost souls. The lurid glare of Hell flickers up before the eyes at this time, the horror of despair, the groans of the damned. The Church points to all this, white with terror, laying hold upon ungodly souls, and crying with a mother's agonising voice, "Flee for thy life."

She does well, and her terror is infectious, and persuades some to flee from the wrath to come. And yet she is stronger and more persuasive, and her harvest of souls is yet greater when she rather allures by love, and wins by promises, and is mighty in gentleness, and displays the mother's unconquerable patient love that she learnt of Jesus at the foot of the Cross.

Let this then be our Advent thought to-day; the coming of Jesus as He went away, blessing; the wondrous thought of the good things He has prepared, and the yet more wondrous thought for each soul to appropriate to itself, "All this for me; for me! For me a sinner, ungrateful, unworthy, unloving! For me He died! For me He has waited, while I have wandered, and rejected Him, and denied Him, and wounded Him! For me there is yet hope, mercy, salvation!"

Monday after the First Sunday.

RESPONSIBILITY.

As our Lord's ministry drew towards the end, and the Jews not only continued to reject Him, but constantly increased in bitterness and animosity, His teaching steadily increased in severity. He speaks constantly in His parables of judgment and retribution. The barren fig-tree doomed, the foolish virgins shut out, the guest without the wedding garment hurried in shame from the feast, the faithless steward surprised and punished, the servants who had received pounds and talents, and had not made good use of them, terribly dealt with; all this is crowded into the record of the last few days of our Lord's public life, besides His prophecies of the destruction of Jerusalem, and of the end of the world. If we compare His parables at the beginning of His teaching with those at the end, the contrast is very striking; as His own humiliation draws near, He brings out more and more His character of Judge of mankind. And while the Good Shepherd was actually giving His life for the sheep, He dwells, as He had never before done, upon the awful doom of the goats upon the left hand. The lightning flashes of the Second Advent flicker upon the last word-pictures of the rejected Messiah; He sets His face steadfastly towards the Cross, but He seems already to see it gleaming in the heavens, the sign of His second coming, and of the judgment of the world.

It is the fashion of the day to explain away and water down the terrors of the Bible. We may regard the fashion, as we would take any other passing fashion, for what it is worth; but let us take the awful and often-repeated words of the Lord Jesus Himself about judgment and lost souls, and remember what He tells us, notwithstanding men's talk, "My words shall not pass away."

The parable of the Talents was spoken to the apostles, who had received many gifts and high powers to use for Him, while the parable of the Pounds was addressed to the ordinary disciples, reminding them of their common gift, and that they must use it for God, and account to Him for it at last. Some of His chosen ones had received five, or even ten talents, but the crowd of ordinary disciples had all received the same trust, each one pound, and their life-work was to trade with it, and make it more, against the return of their Lord. "Occupy till I come." The Lord goes away; His Talents and Pounds alike are in His servants' hands; He is long gone; the entrusted goods seem to be their own, to do as they will with them; no one comes, no one interferes; time passes, and still He does not return; and then at last and suddenly He is there, and calls each to account. "After a long time the Lord of those servants cometh, and reckoneth with them."

This is one great Advent thought, responsibility; responsibility to God. Life takes its colour from our ideas of responsibility. We are responsible to human laws; to what is called public opinion; to the circle of our relations and nearest friends; to the custom and usage of the particular occupation in which we are engaged; to our own conscience; and last and above all, but often practically least of all, to Almighty God, our Maker, our Master, our

RESPONSIBILITY.

Judge. There is a perpetual internal rebellion against responsibility in all these forms and relations. Human pride rebels; the innate lust for liberty rebels; the passions rebel, and often break loose and trample down all thoughts of responsibility, all restraints, and run mad riot, blindly, recklessly, daring the inevitable to come on and do its worst. Our prisons, our workhouses, our hospitals, our asylums, are peopled with those who have rebelled against responsibility, and have been defeated, and lie like the wounded upon the battle-field, suffering for their temerity. Civilised man, for his own protection and for the protection of the institutions he holds dear, has laid down written and unwritten laws. The former are in the Statute Book, the latter guide public opinion. The life and the particular actions of each individual are responsible to these codes of laws, and their violation involves punishment. The temptations of money, the impulses of anger or revenge, the stirrings of the animal instincts, these drive men on to forget or ignore their responsibility to law, and lead them to crimes that the judge must deal with. The wayward fancies of eccentric persons, the pride that will be singular, because it can in no other way gain attention; sometimes the unrestrainable ebullitions of genius, these defy the customs and fashions of the day, and involve men and women in the refined tortures which outraged society visits upon its opponents. Nature has her laws and punishments; the young, the sensual, the energetic, take liberties with their health, and hope to evade their responsibility to the consequences of their transgressions; but retribution comes, and medical men tell us how much sickness is self-sought, and that many men may be said to kill themselves rather than die natural deaths.

Our lives, in their general drift, and in the particular details of their incidents year by year and day by day, are regulated by our sense of responsibility to those near to us. The unmarried man is without the responsibilities of the husband and the father. One son leaves home and settles in a distant country, and never returns; another foregoes marriage that he may maintain and protect a parent, or sisters, or pay debts, or carry out a cherished work that demands all his time and thoughts. The professional man feels himself bound by the etiquette of his order, and in his labours considers the interests of his clients. Every man and woman is influenced in what they do and leave undone, by the judgment and known opinion and wishes of those immediately around them. Besides all this, there is a man's own conscience, his standard of duty, of right and wrong; he refers to this constantly, and regulates his life and actions by its decisions. In all these ways, and in many more that might be instanced, individual liberty is modified by responsibility, and men are forced, not merely to consider what they like, but what they ought to do; not merely gratification but duty.

Now Advent introduces another responsibility. All these other responsibilities remain, but Advent reminds us of our relations to God, and of the reckoning there must be one day with Him. But this responsibility is often forgotten by those who acknowledge their obligations in other directions. One reason for this is, that there is no present sign of God's interference in the maintenance of His rights. This is, it seems, a necessary part of our trial. It is spoken of by inspired writers as leading men to forget or postpone their duty to God. We are told that men will say that all things continue, and therefore will continue, as they were and are; looking at the law, and forgetting the Law-maker. It comes out in the parables one after another. The Steward becomes wasteful, idle, dishonest, just because his lord delays his coming. The recipients of the Talents and of the Pounds alike are left to themselves; their lord goes quite away, they hear nothing of him; there are no messages, no inquiries, no investigations; they seem to be their own masters; their master's goods seem to have become really their own. It is not till after a long time that the day of reckoning comes. So the Bridegroom tarries so long that he is unexpected when he appears; and the apparent security of the world before the Flood, and of Sodom before its destruction, are specially referred to by our Lord as foreshadowing the state of men's minds with regard to His coming again to judgment.

The season of Advent gives us a new motto of life, "Occupy till I come." All that we have, and all that we are, is held on trust, and the period of the trust is our whole life. Human laws, the laws of society and of nature, work out their retribution speedily, but God waits. Our money belongs to God; yet we may hoard it, squander it, withhold all or most of what we are expected to give to God's work in the world, and the fate of Ananias and Sapphira is not ours; we go on smiling and untouched. Our time is God's; yet we may use it all for ourselves, we may let it lapse away, we know not how, till the end comes, and we pass away with none to thank us, none to regret us; but all along the path of our life there will be no voice from heaven, such as Elijah heard when he fled from duty, "What doest thou?" Our bodies, our faculties, our talents, our influence, our natural gifts, all belong to God; we are but tenants-at-will, we occupy till He comes;

but up to the last moment we seem to be free, lords of ourselves; we say "Who is lord over us?" and no one stands forth, no one challenges our liberty, till He comes.

It is the same with the faithful servant. The lawless break out into rebellion while the lord is absent; they burn and destroy, they riot and do what they list; meanwhile the diligent servant is plodding on quietly with his work, and no one praises him; he has trials and losses, no one consoles him. Good and bad alike are let alone by God. This is our situation at this moment. So many years ago we received the Pound, human life, with its ordinary duties, its ordinary responsibilities. So many years yet remain to us, and we may do almost as we like as regards God. We boast of our freedom; we say that an Englishman's religion is between himself and his God. Well and good; but the Englishman was not left out when the word went forth, "Occupy till I come." There will be an end of this absolute liberty. Responsibility may seem to be in abeyance, but it is not extinct. Each one of us has a Master, and the day is drawing near when He will come and reckon with us, and will reward or punish us as we have used that which was always His, but which He left in charge with us for a few years, our Life.

Tuesday after the First Sunday.

WAITING FOR CHRIST.

THE Church's position in Advent might be briefly described in the words of St. Paul, "Waiting for the coming of the Lord Jesus Christ." But in truth this is the attitude of the godly in all ages. All through the Bible God's people speak of themselves as "waiting." Even as far back as the time when Noah was born, we find men waiting and looking forward. Jacob, blessing his twelve sons, interrupts himself in the midst to say, "I have waited for Thy salvation, O God." All the prophets have similar expressions. David's psalms are so full of the same thought that they have been daily used by the Church, as expressing her position, and that of all true Christians, "Waiting for the coming of our Lord Jesus Christ." As soon as sin came into the world, men began to long and wait for the coming Saviour. The godly succession has never been broken. There was a never-failing line of faithful souls, up to Simeon and Anna, who waited daily in the temple for the Consolation of Israel, and who there found Him to their exceeding joy, and then were content, and said, "Lord, now lettest Thou Thy servant depart in peace, for mine eyes have seen Thy salvation."

But soon the Christ departed again from the world. A little while He was seen, and then for a little while He withdrew Himself, and the old attitude was taken up again. The New Testament corresponds with the Old;

the faithful are still " waiting for the coming of our Lord Jesus Christ." The Old Testament closed with a promise of the coming of the Son of Man; the New Testament closes with the same promise, " Surely I come quickly; Amen;" and the prayer of the Church follows, " Even so, come, Lord Jesus." Daily the prayer goes up from thousands of Christian lips and hearts, " Thy kingdom come;" daily, nay unceasingly day and night, the cry of the martyrs and waiting saints in Paradise is heard before God, " Lord, how long?" Each time the faithful come together they say, " I believe that Jesus Christ shall come again to judge the quick and the dead." Each time the Holy Eucharist is celebrated, " His death is shown forth till He comes again," so says the Apostle. " This do in remembrance of Me;" in remembrance of My death; to keep up the remembrance of Me absent, but coming again.

Such is the attitude and position of the Church; she is a constant witness for Christ come and for Christ coming; a witness against the world, which wishes to forget God, and to live in and be satisfied with the present; a witness that all things shall come to an end; an unwelcome witness, to a busy, self-pleasing world, that there is a day coming when the Judge shall call mankind to give an account of words and works, of days and years.

This word "waiting" expresses the state and condition of the Church in all times and in all places; at Corinth in St. Paul's day, and in England now. And what is true of the Church is true also of every sincere and faithful member of it. He or she is now and always " waiting for the coming of our Lord Jesus Christ." Let us think what this means; how are we to wait? Nay, let us see whether we really are waiting at all.

First, then, the true servant of God waits for Christ as his judge. This is what the Creed specially insists upon ; " He shall come again to judge the quick and the dead." Oh, that strange, awful day when all men shall rise again from death ! Troops and myriads of men and women and children from all countries and all ages of the world, multitudes that no man can number, bewildering multitudes; and yet each alone before God, each a distinct and separate and responsible soul ! As each individual human face is distinct and peculiar, and there is no other face quite like it, so each soul is distinct, and stands alone in the presence of God, its Maker, as if there were but it alone and God. There will be no shelter for any soul because of the vast, numberless crowd. The eye of God will meet every eye, and each reasonable soul will read its just and unalterable doom in His face. All thoughts and words and deeds will be seen in a moment. Here there is some light indeed, but there are hiding-places; we cannot see or be seen as we are. Then there will be light, pervading, penetrating light, and we shall be seen, and we shall see ourselves as we are; and every one by his own conviction, and the assent of the assembled hosts of angels and men, shall "go to his own place." No need of long trial ; no need of witnesses and defence; every man's life will be read in his face. If he has truly repented, his sins will have been washed away by the Blood of the Lamb, and he will stand pure and blameless before the Judge, and will be acknowledged as a son of God, having the likeness of God in himself, and will claim his birthright, and enter his eternal home, God and angels and men and devils seeing the justice of his pretensions. If he has not repented ; if his sins have been persevered in, and loved, and hidden ; if they have been too sweet and too dear to be broken off; if the man or the woman has been too busy, or too idle, or too careless to get pardon in the way that has been provided; if the voice calling to repentance has been so often heard and disregarded, that by and by it ceased to have influence, and death has come, and with it the end of the day of grace, then that soul will stand filthy and sin-laden before the Judge, and before angels and men and evil ones, and before its own shamed and terror-stricken eyes; and then of its own free will, convicted by its own consciousness and the evidence of all, it will turn away to its own place, the abode of evil, where God is not.

All this is before the eye of the godly man, all this is in his heart, as he waits for the coming of the Lord Jesus Christ. If he is surprised by sin, he hastens to repentance, lest the day of Christ should come, and he should have that sin unpardoned upon his soul, and so after all be lost. If temptation is strong, and he is weak and is on the point of yielding to the sweet irresistible delight, the thought comes, "I may die in the midst of this, and no repentance be possible for me," and so he can turn away, and be safe. If sins long ago committed, the sins of youth, sins lightly thought of at the time, come up to his mind, some ray of light from the face of God penetrating the dark record-chambers of his soul, he thinks of the day of light that shall reveal all; he fears lest he may not have truly repented, he fears lest he may have been too easy with himself; he will go over his life again on his knees, and confess all; he will not fear to seek the aid of God's ministers, as the apostles and the Church recommend; he thinks little of pain and shame now, so that he may be clean, a pardoned soul, at the coming of the Lord Jesus Christ. His one dread is unpardoned sin. He is waiting for Christ's coming; it may be upon him at any moment. Sin is ever surprising him, coming in upon him from without, or breaking out upon him from within; he dare not make light of it; he dare not leave it alone; he must confess it, and be rid of it as soon as he sees it, lest the Judge should come suddenly, and he be convicted, and taken with the accursed thing evidently upon him.

Thus waits the godly man; thus he cleanses his soul day by day, just as the filth of the world requires him day by day to cleanse his body. Thus he is diligent in prayer; thus he comes to the Table of his Lord, to strengthen and refresh and support his soul, just as the wear and tear of work forces him to eat and drink and sleep, that his body may be supported and live.

But the godly man waits also for the coming of the Lord Jesus Christ, as for a master. Even a bad servant works diligently when his master's eye is upon him. We may often see idle, dishonourable workmen, who have been robbing their master by wasting time when his back was turned, set to work with wonderful energy when they see him coming. Now the godly man always sees his Master coming. The voice of the Church constantly says in his ears, "The Lord is at hand." Whatever then his hand findeth to do, he does it with all his might. He goes to his daily work in shop or warehouse or elsewhere, as the servant of Christ; he takes his daily task from Christ's hand; he believes that He has made him what he is, placed him where he is. He is "diligent in business," because he is "serving the Lord." No human eye perhaps may ever see a certain act of idleness or dishonesty, or dishonourable dealing, but what of that? He knows that his Master is coming, that He knows all, and that for this he will certainly be called to account. He may not be as successful as he could wish; he may not be as comfortable, as congenially placed and employed as he thinks he might be, but he is where his Master has put him; it is only for a little while; his Master is coming, and it will soon be over; and so he plods on, and if he cannot be quite happy and contented, at least he is patient and hopeful, for he knows how it is written that "many that are last shall be first, and the first last." He believes that if in lowly place he serves well, his Master may bid him "come up higher." There is other work too; work not for self, but for God, and for His Church, and for his fellow-men; and the godly man is not content, he does not feel safe, unless he is doing something of this kind. And because after all he cannot do all he would like to do, he is glad to help those who are doing those good works; and so he is liberal with his money; he is glad to give Sunday by Sunday at the offertory, because he knows that he will have a share in the blessing which it will bring upon all who are on God's side, and are doing Christ's work of mercy in this world of sin and sadness.

There is a great deal more that might be said about the godly man's waiting for the coming of our Lord Jesus Christ; but let us notice only one other aspect of this waiting. The true Christian waits for Christ as for his dearest Friend and his most loving Saviour. Have we not sometimes heard or read of some good man, till we wished very much indeed we could see him and speak to him? Have we not sometimes wished we could have lived in the old gospel days, and sat and listened to the words of Jesus, and looked into His dear face, and touched the hem of His garment? And when we think of His death upon the Cross, and know that it was for us; and when we remember all God's goodness and mercy to us all the days of our life, is it not a good thought, and one that makes our heart warm and beat, to think that there will be a day when we shall indeed see Jesus Christ; the very face that was turned upon Peter, the very hands that blessed those little children, the very body that hung upon the Cross, and that the disciples saw in the upper chamber when He lifted up His nail-printed right hand and blessed them? Is it not pleasant to meet old friends who have been long away from us? But what friend is like Him, for whose coming we are waiting? Is it not a wonderfully comforting thought for mourners, to think of seeing again those whom God has taken to Himself, whom they loved so much? But who ever loved us as He loved us? Who has been faultless, full of all lovableness, without one drawback, as He is, for whom we are waiting? Day after day passes, week after week, year after year; we wait, and the time is shortening; the end, the meeting, is coming on, the meeting of Jesus and the soul which He loved so well that He died for it; the end of trial, of danger, of sin; the home prepared by a Father for His sons and daughters; the realising at last that greatest, that one worthy joy of the human soul, to love and be loved, without one doubt, without a hindrance, purely, perfectly, eternally.

Wednesday after the First Sunday.

OPPOSITION TO CUSTOM.

IN the East all change is disliked and feared; what is customary is favoured; what is new is esteemed wrong, or at least suspicious. The rule is that people must do as their fathers did before them. The same customs, the same names, the same dress, the same laws and governments, these must be observed and maintained; novelties, revolutions, and what we call "progress," these must be avoided. In many parts of the East at the present day human life is going on unchanged in the same routine as was followed in the days of Abraham. All attempts to force western ideas upon orientals have hitherto failed. Thus a recent writer says, "The charm of a visit to the East is the absence of intellectual life there, the freedom one's mind gets from anxiety in looking forward, or pain in looking back. Nobody here thinks of the past or of the future, but only of the present." China with its vast population, its cold religion, its national education, its intelligence and civilisation, declines to adopt European principles, and having weighed and appraised them with care, has decided that its own are best, and tend most to the welfare and happiness of mankind. Our restless eager theories at once set this down as crass stupidity, but grave and thoughtful men know that there is much more to be said for the old ideas than is commonly thought. We make much of the results of the steam-engine and the printing-press, but we keep out of sight the modern evils, the new miseries that have come in the train of what we call "civilisation." If the greater happiness of the greater number is the chief good; if high intellectual culture in the few is believed to be less valuable than the material comfort and content of the great bulk of the people, untortured by restless desires that can never be satisfied; then we have but gained a loss by our vaunted discoveries and advancement; and the unprogressive races of mankind have chosen the wiser course.

But with this question we have not to do just now. It is more impossible for us to go back than for others to go forward. We have launched upon a swiftly running stream, and now, whether we will or not, we are carried forward. We have adopted a system, and now the system has fairly mastered us, and we must arrive at the conditions which will be evolved by it, whether they involve our happiness or our misery.

But while this is so, and while changes are applauded by us when they have been made and are successful, it is as true with us as with orientals that deviation from present custom and fashion is regarded with horror and suspicion. People follow one another like sheep. Dress is a minor but most patent instance. The fashion of to-day will be as intolerable ten years hence as the fashion of ten years ago would be to-day; but to-day to-day's fashion must be adopted. Nobody seems to know where or with whom the authority resides, or who regulates what people should wear; but there are Christian women less afraid of moral transgressions than they are of the transgression of the passing fashion in the cut of their clothes. Society tolerates violation of God's laws with great composure, but is cruelly vindictive against those who break its unwritten and ever-changing laws.

All real reformation, every improvement, has had to fight its way against this dead weight of fashion, custom, and prejudice. Things most common, most useful now, absolutely necessary to us, as we suppose, have had to face opposition the most determined and the most bitter, and that in many cases but a few years ago. A French proverb says that it is the first step that is the most difficult and the most costly, and it is a fact that every step of the marvellous advance that has been made in Europe for some centuries has cost its originators something that is dearest and most precious to man. One sows, another reaps; men mostly sow in tears, that happier generations may reap in joy. Such has been the history of Christianity itself. Its novelty was its original condemnation; its opposition to received religious customs led to its being called atheism. If a man became a Christian, he was charged with disrespect to the memory of his ancestors and the opinions and practice of his relations and friends. The very first article of the Church's charter was separation. The word church, "ecclesia," means something that is called out, separated. Our Lord's call of His apostles, His charge to them, His rules for their guidance, all expressed more or less separation from the world. He set himself in opposition to the world, and declared it his enemy. His forerunner, St. John Baptist, severed himself from common life, and from birth to death lived apart. Food, clothing, place of abode, everything about him indicated separation, not merely from kinsmen and friends, but from the world and its customs and ways, till his death sealed his testimony in the most striking manner; for while he was secretly and without honour or witness suffering death in a dungeon, Herod was keeping birthday feast with good cheer and merry company and music and dancing, and all that the world and human nature desire and enjoy.

Nor did this begin even with the Baptist. The Israelites were called out and separated from other nations; their charter had for its first and fundamental article national purity. Their privileges and promises depended entirely upon their keeping themselves absolutely apart from all the world, isolated, distinct, unapproachable. And all this dated yet further back, to the time when the father of the faithful was called out of his country and from his father's house to wander homeless through the world, to live and to die an exile from his native land, with no inheritance in the world but a grave. Perhaps we may go back earlier still, and understand what is said in Genesis of men beginning to "call themselves by the name of the Lord," as an indication that in the primitive ages, when human principles of life were developing and foreshadowing the course that was to be followed by empires and by individuals, these God-fearing men with wise prescience foresaw what was coming, and enrolled themselves under the name of God instead of under the title of family or tribe, or mighty ruler of men. And so each man had his own name, not the name of his kindred or ancestor, but a name that bore in it some letters of the name of God, Elohim or Jehovah, indicating the man's subjection to God, and that he placed His commands before those of custom, or family, or king.

What, then, is all this to us? Time would fail if we attempted to quote the many words of our Lord and His apostles as to the perpetual maintenance of this spirit of separation between the disciples of Christ and the world at large. The purity and vitality of the Church has ever depended upon it; when it has been forgotten or violated the Church has suffered and become dead or corrupt. It was the mighty working of this great thought, the compelling influence of this divine truth, that in the early ages of Christianity drove men and women to the deserts to live separate lives—lives of spiritual altitude, which they despaired of attaining in the midst of the universal corruption of the world. It was the same deep conviction that led to the yet happier venture of Benedict and his blessed sons, who in heart separate from the world yet lived in its midst, and by their magnificent virtues, their noble and unwearied labours, converted it. They gave their lives for their brethren, and they saved them. They transformed savage chiefs into Christian kings, desolate wastes into smiling fields, fruitful of corn and wine. Their lonely huts became noble cities; their rough wooden oratories, stately cathedrals; their humble schools, world-famed universities. It was the spirit of separation that wrought these great results; these men ruled others, because they had first conquered themselves; they governed the world, because they had already renounced it, and taken a higher rule for their guidance. In modern times the world seems to be rejecting Christianity, triumphing over the Church. Is it because the Church is untrue to her ancient principles, and has given up her ancient and divine method of practice? If new reformers arise, will they not be like the old reformers, like all true reformers, separate men, men working on the old lines?

"Themselves first training for the skies,
They best will raise the people there."

The masses of population in our large towns, multitudes ignorant of the very name of God except as an expletive for cursing, apostates from the faith, the deluded followers of fanatics, demagogues, and self-interested intriguers; the victims of drink, of disease, of hereditary degradation, the hopeless residuum of wrecked lives and ruined characters, the miserable offscouring of nineteenth century humanity; he who will save these, must not think of saving himself. Is it not because there are so few great saints that there are so many great sinners?

In like manner for each individual soul there is need of perpetual reminding of this principle of separation as fundamental and essential to the Christian life. There is a never-ceasing tendency to lapse into conformity to the world, to pare away differences, to give up peculiar practices, to do like the rest. There is a constant remonstrance, "Do as other people do; there is no one now-a-days that is so strict and particular; do not make yourself peculiar and conspicuous. Why do you suppose you know better than other people? Why do you pretend to be so much more religious than your neighbours and relations?" Who has not heard such things, either as argument, or taunt, or sneer? Who has not been influenced by words such as these? Who is not afraid of what people will say? How many are even now keeping back from what they know is right, only because they dare not be different from those about them. One is holding back from Holy Communion; many are unwilling to attend week-day services; others will not give a little time to work for God, or His Church, or the poor; and more still cannot make up their minds to give up some habit, some practice, some indulgence; while here and there there are souls called to the higher Christian life, who stifle the voice that ever speaks within them, and go on still upon the lower, less noble way, because so many keep them company therein.

Of course it is not meant that we should affect singularity, or mistake eccentricity for genius or high spirituality. Our Lord and His Apostles followed the customs and fashion of their day as far as they were lawful or immaterial. But when the world says and does one thing, and God plainly commands another, then it is that choice must be made, and is made.

Here, then, is a rule and precept for us, most wholesome, most necessary in these days. The servant of God is a good subject of Cæsar so long as Cæsar does not command him to render to him the things of God. The Christian is a good citizen, but the voice of the Church, or of his own conscience, sometimes compels him to be in opposition to his fellow-citizens. Christ teaches filial obedience, and would have men to be of one mind in an house, but this paramount law of putting God first and man second has caused and does cause, as He said it would, a man's foes to be those of his own household, son against father, brother against brother. When our duty is clear, we must not mind the way of the world, nor custom, nor fashion, nor the practice and habits of neighbours, and relations, and friends, but must just go our own way, and take the consequences.

God's call to the soul is, and ever has been, " Hearken, O daughter, and consider, incline thine ear; forget also thine own people and thy father's house; so shall the King have pleasure in thy beauty: for He is thy Lord God, and worship thou Him." The soul is the bride of God; it gives up its own name, and takes His; it sacrifices its own liberty, and takes His will for its own. There are degrees of separation from the world, and of union with

God, some being called to higher spirituality than others; but no one is altogether exempt from the call to separation. "As much as lieth in you, live peaceably with all men." But let us remember, that when God says one thing and men another, we must obey God rather than men.

𝕿hursday after the 𝕱irst Sunday.

THE ANNIHILATION OF SIN.

ST. PAUL'S prayer for his converts at Corinth was that they might be "blameless in the day of our Lord Jesus Christ." "The day of our Lord Jesus Christ;" the great, wonderful, terrible day to which all days are gravitating, to which all men are drawing near, ready or unready, willing or unwilling, with open and expectant face, or face averted, like Lot's wife, looking impotently back. Among all mankind, in all ages and in all places, there has been a sense more or less acute of the sure coming of such a day. Men have argued against it, sneered, ridiculed, ignored it, but there has still remained the impression that after all there will be such a day. Good and bad, careful and careless, Christian and heathen, learned and rude, ancient and modern, mankind's verdict at last is that such a day will come, and that every eye that once has seen the light of the sun will see also the ineffably brighter light of that great day. Doubtless the knowledge of it was given at the beginning; doubtless, too, the truth became obscured, perverted, forgotten, till Christ came and declared again the old revelation, and enlarged it, and made it plainer. And now the judgment to come, the judgment of men by a Man, the judgment of each severally, words, deeds, omissions, all the intricate maze of actions, and circumstances, and relations that makes up the life of each of us, this stands out as a fixed article of Christian faith, upon which those who differ much in other points all agree.

The sense of this affects us almost unconsciously and continually. There is the greatest possible difference in our feelings when we know that we are quite free and irresponsible, and when we know that we are accountable to another for what we are doing. This is so even in little things. If our work is to be scrutinised by another, the idea accompanies us all along its execution. Thrust it aside as we may, ignore it, drown it in more agreeable thoughts, rationalise against it as we may, there will come in day by day unbidden, unwelcome often, unexpectedly, unaccountably, the conviction that we have not done with our words and our acts, but that we shall meet them again in "the day of our Lord Jesus Christ."

"His day" indeed. Now He has not His own; His rights are trampled down; His claims are ignored; but then He will be the one object of all attention, the arbiter of the eternal fate of all and each. It will be "His day" then, without rival, without question, without appeal.

And what of us? What will be our state and condition? How shall we prepare for that day? What shall we aim at? How shape our course with regard to that, the great momentous end of all? There have been many replies, and many theories put forth in the world's wisdom. Some have said, "Live by nature; do as your natural instincts bid you; and then stand forth boldly and say to your Judge, 'What harm have I done, for I am as Thou hast made me? I have lived as the impulses which Thou didst implant within me led, or drove, or biassed me; acknowledge and approve Thine own work.'" Other some, "Your lower nature is vile; crush it, beat it down, let the pure spirit alone rule and master; once slip, once yield, and all is gone; only the spotless, unearthly spirit can enter the abode of spiritual purity."

Others have taught otherwise, this way and that way; for the teachers have been many, and the theories and systems manifold.

But what says the great Teacher, He who alone knows, for He has ordained all the circumstances of that day? Time would fail to detail all that He has revealed. Let us, then, take only one idea, which seems to sum up all the rest, and which His Apostle, St. Paul, sets before us in the words already quoted. In one word he describes the attitude and condition in which souls may stand before their Lord and Judge in that day; and that word is a singular and unexpected one, "blameless." The idea seems to be this: the Great Assize is sitting; the accuser is there; he details against the soul sins deadly, numberless; he makes out a clear and unanswerable case, there can be no reply; he has proved sins of commission and omission, sins of infirmity and of wilfulness, sins done with each faculty of body, soul, and spirit; and now, in final demonstration, he demands that all look upon that soul, that all may see in it the traces, and marks, and evidences of everything that he has described; for in that world and in that searching light there is nothing secret, nothing hid, nothing past, but each soul bears upon its own face its own history, readable like a book. And lo, as men and angels turn and look upon that shrinking soul, it is evident to them, it is evident to itself, it is evident to its accuser, that it is "blameless." The sins are not denied, but the evidence of their committal is absolutely wanting; the soul stands just before the eye of justice, and the verdict of all the assessors is instant and unanimous, "Blameless, blameless! Who can lay anything to the charge of God's elect?"

Such will be the state of the blessed in the day of the

Lord Jesus Christ; such is the condition which the Apostle bids us seek and desire and pray for, nay, obtain against that day. Those to whom he is writing are not without sin; he urges them to purity and holiness, and a high and superhuman standard of life; but while he urges it, he sees them failing, except in some blessed, exceptional instances; but for all, highest and lowest, saint and penitent, Christian child and converted adult, the fallen and oft relapsed, and the faithful and consistent alike, he holds out one ideal, he hopes and prays for nothing higher for any than that in that day they may be "blameless."

How is this mystery effected? We began with one article of our Creed, that our Lord Jesus Christ "shall come again to judge the quick and the dead;" we must go to another article for the key to this mystery of blamelessness, "I believe the forgiveness of sins." These words are few, but they are deep and wonderful, and utterly inexplicable. The forgiveness of sin, as taught by Christ and His Church, is a mystery quite above all understanding. It is not what we mean when we say we forgive those who trespass against us; the thing is there still, only we agree to say no more about it, to take no steps with respect to it, to pass it by, and, as far as may be, forget it. But it is not so that God forgives sin. A forgiven sin is annihilated, destroyed: and to destroy anything is as much the sole attribute of God as to create. We cannot create anything; we may make something out of other things, but God alone can create; so we cannot destroy anything. We may put something into the fire, for instance, and a change passes upon it, its elements are separated, its form disappears, but it has only undergone a chemical change; carbon and gases will account for every particle of it; we have not destroyed one single atom of matter. God alone can destroy; He alone who inhabiteth eternity, to whom all time is but one present moment, He alone can undo the past, and make it not to be; and this He does in the pardon of sin. He does not forget; He does not cover it up and say nothing about it; He does not turn it into something else, but he annihilates it. And the means and instrument by which this is done is the Precious Blood of Christ, the divine absolution. "If we confess our sins, He is faithful and just to forgive us our sins." So mighty a result from so small a means! What, the pardon of sins so easy? Dare we tell the whole truth? Will it not make men careless and encourage them to take liberties with God? Yes, it may, and it does; yet the truth must be told, and the consequences must be left with God. The way of pardon is open to all, free, easy, day by day, week by week, year by year; and at last, if it may be, upon the dying bed, the earnest Christian seeks the application of the Precious Blood to his sin-stained soul, that in the day of our Lord Jesus Christ he may be found "blameless."

If, then, the way of salvation is so plain and easy, how is it that any miss it? How is it that any are lost? How indeed? Simply because they will not use the one remedy. Sin is not confessed, and therefore is not forgiven. Sin is loved, and clung to, and persisted in, till death comes and seals all up for ever. Men and women are too busy, or too indolent, or too careless to set about the work of repentance. The sins of youth are forgotten, but they are not forgiven; they lie within upon the soul like some slow, uncured sore upon the body that we hide, and none knows but ourselves. While some are so living and so dying, unpardoned, while the Precious

Blood is running to waste close at hand, others, side by side with us, are quietly going day by day to the ever-flowing fountain of the Precious Blood, and they wash and are cleansed. They are sinners as we are; they have faults and infirmities, they seem perhaps worse on the whole than we, only they never cloak their sins; they never lie down at night till the day's transgressions have been laid at the foot of the Cross, within reach of the drip of the Precious Blood. And so they are washed, healed, and justified now; and in the day of the Lord Jesus they will be found "blameless."

Friday after the First Sunday.

BALAAM'S PRAYER.

THE history of Balaam is one that not only strikes us by its picturesque and poetical features, but which perplexes and baffles us by its mystery and difficulties. To make the history of Balaam useful to ourselves we must strip off on both sides all temporary and personal peculiarities, and must place ourselves side by side with him on the broad basis of a common humanity. We can never know what the exact relations were that existed between man and His maker in those old-world times; but we are sure that man then as now had that mysterious conscience that accuses or excuses. We cannot know what power Satan exercised by means of idolatrous worship and magical rites, but we can stand on common ground when we find this man hesitating between duty and self-interest, between an inward and immovable sense of God's justice and the relation of actions here to another life hereafter, and an unconquerable lust for the present gratification of some master-passion that subjects all our impulses to its iron will; and we can understand why two Apostles warn us to beware of the way of Balaam.

Although there is so much that is utterly foreign to us in the story of Balaam, there are words and thoughts and acts that come home to our very heart of hearts, and we seem to see ourselves, past, present, or possible, painted to the life, reflected as in a mirror. Those famous words of his still pulsate with life, they rise to our lips almost as if they were our own, the offspring of our own hearts; we too have often thought, if we have not said, "Let me die the death of the righteous, and let my last end be like his."

Who is there who has not sometimes godly feelings, high and heavenly aspirations? Who does not bow in loving reverence before the majesty of truth, the nobility of true godliness? Who does not sometimes rise in spirit above all the littlenesses of this life, all the unsatisfying pleasures of sense, and aspire in his better self to some higher life, to some more worthy home, to some perfect ideal of all that is great and good and true and beautiful and loving? But what of this? Does this represent our self, our very inner self? We probably try and persuade ourselves that it does. Do we not remember moments of exaltation as we remember the bright days of the past, and forget all the everyday monotony so different, so inferior? Do we not take the exceptional features in our retrospect of life as if they were our life itself; as the traveller, looking back, sees only the hill-tops, but none of the long weary level miles between? If it be so, do we not forget that the true value of our character and of our life must be measured like the strength of a chain, by its weakest not its strongest link? We know our duty so well that we get at last to fancy that we do it as a matter of course. We keep up a respectable, if not even a godly, exterior; we use good words; and men take us very much at our own price, till we cannot believe the unwelcome and half-stifled voice of conscience that tells another tale, and fixes our moral worth at a far lower estimate. Those time-hallowed prayers and praises that the Church puts into our mouth, words of penitence, words of hope, words of praise and joyous thanksgiving, are our souls always really in harmony with these words? They are quite familiar, but are they real to us? Are they our own?

Have we ever thought of this? Or do we always take it for granted that we can enter into the spirit of the Church's worship on earth, and so be fit, when the time comes, to join with her in heaven? Is it not with us in this matter as it is when we frequently read the description of some place that we have never seen, or of some event long passed, till at length we can scarcely separate our own actual experience from the creations of the imagination, thus made almost real to us? We are as those who wake from sound sleep and vivid dreams, we scarcely know what is real and what is dream; the two are interchanged, or substituted the one for the other. Self-love ever disposes us to keep our eyes fixed upon the best points of our character and history, to the exclusion of the more common phase. We take our inner life for granted, on the strength of the fair face of our outward man, and resent unwelcome warning, or self-searching exhibitions of the mirror of truth, as insulting and injurious.

Balaam had religious knowledge; he had religious feelings; he spoke most religious words; and yet somehow he found himself on his unrighteous way to earn the gold of Balak. In the Prophet Micah we have some other words of his, very noble words indeed. Balak, in fear and trembling, asks what yet more costly sacrifice he shall give besides these sevenfold offerings of bullocks and rams, repeated upon every high hill: "Will the Lord be pleased with thousands of rams, with ten thousands of rivers of oil; shall I give my firstborn for my transgression, the fruit of my body for the sin of my soul?" In reply to this, Balaam pronounces the following sublime truth, evangelical as Isaiah himself: "What doth the

BALAAM'S PRAYER. 37

Lord require of thee, but to do justly, and to love mercy, and to walk humbly with thy God?" He was quite convinced of the happiness of the death of the righteous; he had made choice of it for himself, he said; and yet the pen of truth speaks of him as one who pawned his conscience to earn the wages of unrighteousness.

Nor is he the only example given us. There is Herod, who feared John Baptist, and heard him gladly, and yet somehow he became his murderer. There are the multitudes who followed Jesus, and went without food that they might stay with Him, and yet somehow, not long after, they were found crying, "Crucify Him." There are those Scribes and Pharisees, so strict, so devout to Moses and the prophets, so longing for Messiah, and yet when He came they did not know Him; and they slew Him, out of respect to God and His law. There is our Lord's parable of the Sower, and those who heard the word with gladness, and yet somehow did not bring forth any good fruit for harvest-time.

The fault of the prayer lies on the very surface, and yet withal runs into the inmost soul of the man who uses it. It is the *death* of the righteous that he covets, not his *life*. It is the end he wants, without the means. What idle words, then, are these after all! They are like the massy hills and mountains that we think we see in the distance, and lo, a breeze comes, and the whole prospect rolls away, for it is but cloud and mist; or like the dried-up bodies of men long dead, found in the ruins of some buried city, which crumble to dust at a touch. Balaam, moved by the Spirit of God, uttered his own doom against his will. "I shall see Him, but not now; I shall behold Him, but not nigh." This is the way with many who profess to wish for the death of the righteous.

Their religion is always something future, "not now;" their idea of God is always something far off, "not nigh." "The death of the righteous;" yes, it is a goodly thing, a thing to be desired; his end is honourable, joyous. But what has gone before? How came he to get that title of "righteous" by the time of his death?

Have we not listened with delight to beautiful music, the wondrous creation of some great composer, discoursed to our ear by the master-touch of some skilful performer, and as we have listened, have we not longed for his power, envied his facility, and been ready almost to depreciate the greatness of his genius, because it looks so easy to do what he does? It does look easy; it is easy to him; but how came it to be easy? This is the last end of a beginning long ago, of a life-long work, of hours and weeks and years of drudgery, of self-denial, of patience, of indomitable perseverance triumphing over obstacle and difficulty. Just so is the last end of the righteous; it is one with the beginning and the midst; it is the last chapter to which all the book has been tending; it is the statue for which the column has been slowly built, its foundations deep down, quite out of sight. His death is but one event in his life; it must not be separated from that life; we must have both or neither. When shall we learn this truth? In the early Church men refused to be baptized till they lay on their death-bed; living freely and unfettered, yet hoping thus to die the death of the righteous! In the Church of the Middle Ages men in their last hours were borne to some abbey, and with dying lips made their profession, and were enrolled among the members of the Order, and so died arrayed in the garb of a monk, "the habit of religion," as it was called. Times change; customs change; but principles, the principles of thought, the broad relations of man to God on the one hand, and to the world of sin on the other, these change not.

"I die daily," says the apostle; that is the secret of the death of the righteous. It is no new thing; it is but the last act of a long series of similar acts; a death unto sin all the life long, after the example of Christ; or as we read elsewhere, "Keep innocency, and do the thing that is right, for that shall bring a man peace at the last." The life of the righteous is a life of repentance; "the righteous falleth seven times, and riseth again;" for "there is none that sinneth not; he seeth the sword of vengeance long before, and says, I have sinned, and turns back again into the right way." But the ungodly man "goeth on still in his wickedness," blind, self-satisfied, impenitent, till his soul is required of him. Then he sees his sin, but it is too late; and the sword guards the way to the Tree of Life; and there is a sad voice that laments another wasted life, another lost vocation, another soul ruined by its own wilfulness, in spite of Christ's Atonement, and says, "O that thou hadst hearkened to my commandments, then had thy peace been as a river, and thy righteousness as the waves of the sea."

Saturday after the First Sunday.

WHO WILL BE OUR JUDGE?

THE doctrines of the Trinity and the Incarnation seem to some people to be merely hard dogmas, beyond the powers of our understanding, and totally unconnected with our daily duties, and personal hopes and fears. But in truth it is not so. These doctrines lie at the root and foundation of our religion; upon them it rests; from them it springs; up to them we may trace the peculiar features, principles, and practices of Christianity. Without them our faith is liable to be thrown down and carried away with every blast of vain doctrine, just as a rootless tree is prostrated and torn to pieces by the wind; just as the house built on the sand is washed away piecemeal by the flood. This is not mere conjecture, but fact founded on sad experience. When men, or bodies of men, have given up these truths, they never stop there, but soon let go also other truths, "even denying the Lord that bought them." If the root fails, the tree even to its minutest twig and bud must soon be dead. If the foundation gives way, the building with all its parts, its ornament and its usefulness, must be destroyed. Yet the root of the tree is that part which is most hidden. The foundation of the building is laid in secret, and may not be too narrowly scrutinised without danger to the superstructure.

What, then, in fact, is the peculiarity of the Christian religion that distinguishes it from, and sets it above, all other religions? It is that by it we are united to God, made children of God, one with Him, and He with us; not worshippers only, not servants, not even friends of God, but God's children, members of Christ, bone of His bone, and flesh of His flesh. But this could not have been had not Christ become Man and taken our flesh; nor could that which is called the Incarnation have been had there not been three Persons in the Godhead. Christianity teaches " temperance, soberness, and chastity " with a force that no other religion can, because it begins by telling baptized Christians that their bodies are "temples of the Holy Ghost," that their members are " members of Christ." Christianity teaches love and charity, not through human pity and sympathy only, but because in Christ all men are brethren; because Christ suffers when His members suffer; because those who relieve suffering minister to their own flesh and to Christ's own Person. Christianity defends and honours the poor and the weak, because Christ was poor. It mixes itself with daily life, and sanctifies all honest callings, because Christ lived among us and worked among us. Birth and death, marriage and burial, wealth and poverty, pomp and simplicity, youth and age, joy and sorrow, high estate and low, Christianity belongs to all, has sympathy with all, just because its Divine Author was Himself a Man, and knew what was in man, and Himself made man what he is.

By Christ, His only Begotten Son, God revealed Himself to man; revealed Himself as a God of love, having made man that he might love Him—love Him by his reason, seeing His lovely perfections and attributes, love Him by his instinct, seeing and feeling himself to be made in the image of God. God's service must be a service of love, or it cannot be an acceptable service. God is not to be feared, and Jesus loved. If any such distinction were possible, the opposite would rather be the teaching of Christianity; for our Lord says, "The Father judgeth no man, but hath committed all judgment to the Son." To our Father in heaven we are to look only with love; and that we may the more freely do so, without the interference of fear, He has stepped down from the Judgment-seat and put Another there, that we may draw nigh to Him, not as to our Judge, but only as our Maker, our Friend, our Father.

Do we not forget this sometimes? Do we not forget God our Father, and think only of Jesus? But this cannot be pleasing to God. God Almighty would have us love Him, trust Him, cling to Him. All that Jesus taught us of God, by His words and by His own life, was intended to help us to do this; not to shrink away from God, as if He would hurt us; not to try and propitiate His anger with cruel or gloomy rites, or painful sufferings; not to fear Him for His power, or because He was mysterious in His nature, and we could not see or comprehend Him; but to love God, because He is holy and just and good, because He created us to be happy and to enjoy His attributes.

Since the Fall man is naturally afraid of God; he feels himself out of harmony with God. God is holy, man is sinful; God is just, man is deserving of punishment; God is almighty, and man is weak and absolutely in His power; God is great and incomprehensible, and man fears that his own little trials and wants and sorrows, and all the infirmities that beset him, which take up so much of his time and thoughts, which form so large a portion of his life, which influence his character and his destiny, that all these are nothing to God, beneath His notice. He feels that his fellow-men make allowances for him, that they understand his position, his difficulties, the influence of circumstances; and the idea comes upon him that God is harder to him than his fellow-men are, that God's judgment is more strict, more unyielding, less equitable, less lenient than his own, or any good man's with respect to other men's faults and failings and sins. And so a sort of bitter fatalism takes possession of his mind. He knows he must be judged by God; he knows God's law is strict; he knows that he has broken it, and the thought creates in his mind a desperate feeling, a fear, an aversion, almost a hatred of God, as if He were unjust to him, expecting more of him than he could possibly perform.

But how very far from the truth is all this. If any, before the revelation of the truth by Christ, lived and died subject to this cruel doubt and fear of God, surely to them Christ went during His three days' absence from this world and preached peace, and assured them of a very different judgment, a very different Judge and tribunal from those they had imagined and feared. But let us not think hard thoughts of God; we have no excuse for them. God has been clearly revealed to us as He is by Jesus Christ; he that hath seen Him hath seen the Father. What He is we may read in the Gospels, His works of mercy, His words of love, His death for our salvation. And it is He who shall be our Judge. God has ordained this, that we may love and trust Him the more; even the worst among us; for it is criminals, not just men, that have most to do with the judge.

See the full force, the depth, the point of this. God knows our fears, He knows that they are groundless and unreasonable; for who would judge us so mercifully, so justly, so equitably as our Father? It is not that He distrusts Himself; it is not that He is not as loving as Jesus Christ; it is not that He does not understand us as well as Jesus Christ; it is not on His own account at all, but only on our account; it is in merciful stooping even to our prejudices; it is in consideration of our fears, groundless though they are, that the Father will not judge us, but has committed all judgment to the Son.

But why should we feel more confidence in Him as our Judge than in God the Father? We have already indicated the reason; God is of another nature from ours, far above us. We fancy that He cannot have perfect sympathy with us; that He cannot be patient and tolerant of all the human considerations that are on our side with respect to our sins. We think that our fellow-man would be a better judge; that he would understand us better, "For who knoweth the things of a man, save the spirit of man which is in him;" that if only a perfectly just man could be found, who would not be misled by passion or prejudice, who would have no personal feeling, no traditional bias, who possessed a knowledge of human nature in all its frailty and in all the intricate maze of its mysterious constitution, without himself being subject to that frailty and imperfection; if only such a one could be found, then to his judgment-seat we might go without fear, and be sure that we should have justice and mercy; and that whether we were acquitted or condemned, every mouth would be stopped, and all must acknowledge that they had received the due reward of their deeds.

Now God knows all this; God knows that we feel this, and in His infinite mercy and love He has stooped to gratify this instinctive feeling; He has given us just such a Judge as we feel we want and can fully trust. "I have exalted One chosen out of the people," He says. "The Father judgeth no man, but hath committed all judgment to the Son, because he is also the Son of Man." "God hath appointed a day in the which He will judge the world by that Man whom he hath ordained." He is Man. "He was in all points tempted like as we are;" "He made proof of our infirmities;" "In all our afflictions He was afflicted." Not only did He create us, and so know our frame, but He clothed Himself with human nature; He lived and walked in the world for thirty-three years; He knows it all by experience. Who could more fitly be the Judge of men?

See, then, the value of the great truth of the Incarnation of the Son of God; see how this great fundamental dogma comes up to light when perhaps we least expect it; just as in nature we may sometimes see the primary rocks, the foundation of the round world, here and there cropping out of the ground, and even standing out in mountain peaks against the clear sky. Jesus is the Son of Man; He has lived in the world; He has seen it, felt it, tasted its sweets, drunk its bitterest bitter even to the dregs; felt the strong seductive influence of temptation; seen the trials and hard lot of this person and that; made proof of the malice and spitefulness of men; known how cruel the world is in its judgment, how fickle, how uneven; how it punishes the less guilty, and winks at the crime of the greater offender; how it favours the secret and judicious sinner, but is indignant with the less cautious; how it ruins one man for a single false step, and pardons another seventy times seven. In a word, Jesus knows the world, and the way of the world, and the heart of man perfectly by His own experience, by His own life and observation in the world as a Man. And He will be our Judge. His tribunal will reverse many a sentence; will make many that are last first, and the first last; will clear up many a mysterious tissue of dark deeds; will give freedom to many a captive, and make many a wounded heart to rejoice.

Let us remember the name that He earned for Himself when He was in the world, "the Friend of sinners;" let us remember how He judged in the case of the woman taken in adultery, in the case of Mary the sinner, in the case of the thief upon the Cross. Let us remember His pardon of Peter, His compassionate excuse for His murderers, His condescension to the infirmity of His disciples, and His speedy pardon of their desertion; let us remember how He sought out the poor man whom the Pharisees cast out of the synagogue, and revealed Himself to him as the Messiah, more clearly and distinctly than He did to less unhappy and unfortunate men; how He saw and honoured the upright heart of Zaccheus, publican though he was, and despised by his countrymen; how He talked patiently with the sinful woman of Samaria; how He discouraged some who would have become His Apostles; how He judged by the heart, rather than by the words and circumstances of men; how He submitted to laws and customs, yet showed that He esteemed them at their real value, and that He Himself judged by wider, broader, deeper rules, and more lasting principles.

This, then, is our Judge. He is God, and knoweth all things that ever we did. He is Man, and knows all that labyrinth of influences, within and without, that makes us what we are, and that bends our lives and actions this way and that. "If our heart condemn us, He is greater than our heart, and knoweth all things." "Therefore judge nothing before the time, until the Lord come, Who both will bring to light the hidden things of darkness, and will make manifest the counsels of the heart." "Wherefore it is with me," says St. Paul, "a very small thing that I should be judged of you, or of man's judgment; yea, I judge not mine own self; for I know nothing about myself, but He that judgeth me is the Lord." "There is nothing hidden that shall not be made manifest," whether it be to our praise or our shame.

Such, then, is the Tribunal that awaits mankind; one that all must confess to be just and upright, one that all will confess so to be hereafter, whether it acquits or condemns them. Heathen without law, Jew by the law, Christian by the gospel, all shall be judged by the Man Christ Jesus, and answer as man to man to the strict scrutiny which shall compare each life with the great principles of justice, honour, and truth, which came from God originally, and have ever and in all places been known to him with greater or less clearness. Soon we shall stand before this Tribunal; and He who was, and is, and will be clothed with human Body, a human mother's Son, will bid us give account of the deeds done in the body.

But there is yet one more proof of God's mercy and love towards us in this matter. We have seen how, to take away our fear and to give us confidence in the justice and goodness of Himself, our Father in heaven has entrusted all judgment to the Son, because He has become Man as one of us. Let us notice another wonder of mercy, to enable us to stand with confidence before that Judgment-seat, and have good hope of acquittal. He who will then be our Judge is now our Friend and Advocate. He has not yet mounted the judgment throne, and now He comes, as it were secretly, to us, and says, in the great love He bears us, "Agree with thine adversary quickly, whiles thou are in the way with him, lest at any time the adversary deliver thee to the Judge." In other words, " If thou comest before me when I sit as Judge of angels and men, I must condemn thee ; for the day of grace will be past, and sin must be punished. Satan will accuse thee ; thine own conscience will convict thee ; I must condemn thee. But now thou mayest escape ; I will plead for thee with God, 'as a man pleads for his friend ;' confess thy guilt to me ; trust me ; judge and condemn thyself ; so shalt thou escape my judgment. My Blood shall now wash away thy sin ; thou shalt be clean, and my justice will acquit thee when I am upon the Judgment-seat and thou in the place of the accused before me."

So has God's mercy "contrived" to help on our salvation. All these ways make it easier, and magnify His mercy. If any are lost, it must be through their own wilfulness, in spite of God's goodwill towards them.

Now, then, while we may, let us arise and go to our Father, and tell Him how we have sinned, and He will prevent our confessions with His loving pardon. Now, while we may, let us betake ourselves to Jesus as He hangs upon the cross, and let His Blood stream upon us, that we may be washed clean from sin ; so shall we not fear His face when He cometh in His own glory, and His Father's, and the holy angels'; when the Son of Man shall be seen in the clouds of heaven, and the great white throne shall be set, and all that ever lived shall be gathered before Him; so shall we not fear when He testifieth to us by His Church, "Surely I come quickly;" but our answer shall be in humble faith and trust, "Amen. Even so, come, Lord Jesus."

Second Sunday in Advent.

PERPLEXITY.

To-day's Gospel is but one instance out of many where our Lord foretells a state of things in the future the very opposite to that anticipated by materialistic philosophers. He and His Apostles tell us of man rebelling more and more against God, and so against all authority, rule, and order; of confusion and misery consequently spreading over the nations of the world, till all culminates in the reign of a mighty conqueror, who sweeps away all old landmarks, laws and customs, and inaugurates a new era on atheistic principles. This mighty master of men is called in Scripture Antichrist, or the "Lawless One." The primitive Church was keenly alive to all this; and in subsequent ages, as some great world-monarch has arisen, or some successful conqueror has waded through blood, ruin, and misery to vast power, or some terrible evil has befallen the Church, men have listened with bated breath, and looked out for Antichrist and the last great battle between good and evil, to be won by Christ Himself personally returning to the world. Many times the words of Christ have seemed to be having their fulfilment before men's eyes. The persecuting Roman Emperors stamping out the Church; the terrible Arian heresy; the incursions of the barbarian hordes utterly effacing the magnificent Roman civilisation, the wonderful result of the labours of a thousand years, and reducing Europe to a wilderness; the marvellous career of Mahomet

and his successors; the awful outbreak of the French
Revolution; the rise and triumphs of Napoleon; all those
events and others display some of the features of the last
time, as foretold by our Lord or the apostles, and were
doubtless anticipations of them, showing their possibility,
the shadows of coming events, partially realising them,
after the manner often found in all God's dealings,
whether in nature or human nature, of which science and
the Bible afford so many instances. Before the person or
the event actually comes there are types and partial
realisations of the idea. The tide advances slowly and
with many apparent pauses, and even recoils, but the
wave pushes higher, now on one point of the shore, now
on another, and by and by it will be seen to have en-
croached all along the line till it brims up everywhere to
high-water mark, and every point is covered.

Just now the signs of the times do not threaten much
in the old ways. There is no great conqueror herding
thousands of unhappy men from home, to die in misery
upon battle-fields. Famine and pestilence and the powers
of nature are not just now so actively destructive as heretofore. Christ's words this Advent do not come home to
us as they have in many Advents in past ages to the
watchful Christian. But they are not without special
significance to us if we will notice them. If there ever
was a time when the reign of lawlessness seemed immi-
nent, it is now. There is everywhere rebellion against
authority; there are principles at work, organisations
of men formed and operating, spreading and gaining
strength, which, if they succeed in their plans, must
absolutely overthrow society to its very foundations, and
bring about a social chaos, which experience shows is the
natural prelude to the opposite extreme, a despotism

effected by some clever, unscrupulous tyrant, some master-spirit and born ruler of men.

There is, moreover, one special characteristic of the last days contained in but one word in to-day's Gospel, and so easily overlooked. Along with the other troubles of the last time there is to be "Perplexity." Surely if other features are wanting or faint just now, this feature is having its turn, and is coming into prominence. Other ages may have been closer anticipations of the times of the end in some respects, but these days are confessedly days of Perplexity. Men have not yet generally given up faith in God; Christianity is still living and working in men's hearts, and is ever spreading, growing, and intensifying. But what attacks are being made upon it on all sides! Arguments, once known only to a few, are now become familiar to all. Difficulties in the way of the acceptance of Christianity are thrown out broadcast in books, magazines, speeches, newspapers. The sensual and godless greedily and gladly clutch at them, as excuses for sin, selfishness, and licence; but better men, whose instincts tell them that there is a God, and that all that Christ teaches is truth, still cannot reply to all this; and the consequence is Perplexity. There is a multitude of sects; there are all sorts of religions, each claiming to be the truth; and the result is Perplexity. Once the *pros* and *cons* of religious controversy were shut up in ponderous tomes, and buried in libraries and colleges; now the same morning newspaper contains an argument that the Roman Church is the only depository of truth, and another that she is the Babylon of the Apocalypse; both arguments are well conducted, both are plausible, both are hard to answer, and the result is Perplexity.

The newspaper does it. No book is too deep or too

costly now-a-days for general circulation. The book indeed is not widely read, but its contents are extracted and reviewed in the newspaper that only costs a penny, and which every one reads. Men are always in a hurry; they do not read books, or go to lectures much, or think deeply; it is a superficial age; but newspapers provide for all this; and side by side with murders, and reports of sins, and trade reports, there is a leading article on the latest freethinking book, or a report of some sceptical lecture, or a review of some new manifesto of the religion of doubt and denial, or a speech of some over-talking apologist who details his opponent's case well and answers it weakly, and so spreads the knowledge of what he wishes to combat. And the result of this is Perplexity.

What more need be said? Shall we think of the state and prospects of our own Church; of the diametrically opposite and utterly irreconcileable schools of thought and teaching within its borders? Shall we enumerate the radical differences and theological controversies of the endless sects of Dissenters, or hear how well it can be shown that the Christ of the Gospels never existed? Or shall we take a wider range and enter upon geological theories; or sit down and listen while learned men argue that there is no God, and that all we see and feel, ourselves included, is mere shadow and delusion? No one, in these days, can be quite out of hearing of these things; and the result is Perplexity. Old arguments and vantage-ground that once held good are failing now. Good orthodox obstinacy, blind bigotry, crass ignorance, deep reverence for authority and for custom, insular prejudice, all these things are shaken; men hear all sides, and the result is Perplexity. Clever men, good men, are to be found with every sort of opinion; men whose judgment deserves respect, and their acts attention, are moving hither and thither, changing sides, embracing controverted opinions; one never knows what will come next, and who will say or do something extraordinary; and the result is Perplexity.

If we take a wider range, politics, commerce, social science, these and other important matters are one and all invaded by the same spirit. Everywhere we see change, novelty, upsetting of old positions and traditions. The future gives rise to apprehension, the present to Perplexity.

Let us, then, seek for the remedy for all this, or rather, perhaps, indicate the spirit in which to meet this temper of the day, and suggest the antidotes to counteract its miserable working in our own hearts and lives. Take we then first of all this thought. All this, that shakes so many in their faith, may be turned into an argument to establish us in it. Who would have imagined that, after 1800 years of the acceptance of Christianity, any would have begun to demand evidences and to doubt? Yet Christ foresaw all this, and it is recorded for us that He foretold of these days that they would be times of Perplexity, and of later days yet, He said, that in them it would be hard to find faith upon the earth; and St. Paul adds that there will be a falling away, a wide and general apostasy from Christianity before the end comes; and the earliest post-apostolic writers speak in the same way, having received this truth with the rest from the days of inspiration. No strange thing is happening unto us then, but just what our Master said would come. In the first age of the Church His servants were made partakers of His Cross by persecution; martyrs and confessors suffered in their bodies. The cross is still laid upon Christians, there is still martyrdom, suffering, pain, and shame for Christ's sake, but now it is mental suffering; the mind is crucified; the dearest hopes, the tenderest emotions of the heart are racked and lacerated; it is these, not the limbs and members of men and women, that are flung to the lions in these days. There is equality between us and the early Christians; they without us cannot be made perfect.

Then let us remember that every truth, however certain, may be spoken against. There are strong arguments against any and every proposition. A child or any other ignorant person may ask some questions which only the very wise can answer, and some which no one can answer. It is always and in everything easier to pull down than to build; easier to destroy than to make. Those who rejected Christ when He was upon earth had strong arguments, reasons, scriptural and otherwise, for doing so. Mathematical certainty is not to be had except in mathematics; and so when people hear for the first time attacks upon what they have always considered unassailable certainties they are perplexed, and sometimes altogether overcome.

Next let us not attach too much importance to the fact that clever and learned men are against us. Clever and learned men are not infallible; they often make egregious mistakes. They are good authorities in their own specialities, but are no better than ordinary men, indeed often less reliable, out of their particular line of study. For example: scientific men proved to their own satisfaction that railway trains could not run twenty miles an hour. Real scientific discoveries, such as those of astronomy and physiology, have been readily accepted by Christians without injury to their faith; we may therefore rest assured that no scientific progress that is founded on truth will ever be found incompatible with Christianity.

Lucretius taught that rugged mountains were such a defect in the beauty of nature, that they were a standing proof that the world was not the work of a Divine Being. Now we travel across Europe to watch the after-glow upon the Alps, and feel our souls lifted up to God as we gaze upon their mighty peaks, and the tremendous glaciers that slowly creep round their bases. It is not merely that our tastes have been developed, but that, our knowledge having been extended, we understand the works of God better.

Again let us not forget that much that is most talked of in these days as upsetting Christianity is by no means proved. The theories are rejected even by many who are no friends of Christianity. They are shown to be mere assumptions, most illogical; and their utter discomfiture and oblivion are confidently expected. Let us not imagine that Christ's enemies are all agreed; they are ready to pull one another to pieces. Just as it was when He was on His trial, so now, their "testimony does not agree together."

We must not too readily accept professions of honesty, as if they who say so were the only lovers of truth; as if they alone were the friends of humanity. There is many a poor man or woman who, by imitating Jesus Christ's loving tenderness, has done more good in their lifetime to suffering humanity than these men who have lived but to exalt themselves, who are brimful of pride and selfishness, and care not who or what suffers, if only they get fame and notoriety as original thinkers and clever men. There is such a thing among men as hatred of God. The vulgar and outspoken secularist or communist expresses it in open words; the gentlemanly professor coins scientific phrases to hide his thoughts. The rebellion of the fallen angels was the revolt of gifted intellects. God has never addressed His revelations to the intellect. Every creature must humble himself before Him.

Lastly, let us be patient. Let us move with caution and slowness. In a fog, or in the thick darkness, men feel here and there before they take each step. A false move will only turn bad to worse. Like St. Paul and the crew of the water-logged ship of Alexandria we must wait and "wish for the day." What is perplexing now may be clear some day; and if not, we must accept the cross that Christ has chosen for us, and believe, not only that it is the best for us, but that it is the only one we can have, and that it is a ladder to lift us to heaven. If theory is perplexing, practical duty is clear; and it is written, "If any man do the will of God, he shall know of the doctrine." This will help us against petulant throwing away of all faith in time of childish impatience or gloomy desperation. There are greater difficulties in infidelity than in belief. It degrades man in his own eyes, turns him into a mere beast, and therefore makes him utterly restless, reckless, and dissatisfied, "wandering aimlessly through the centre of indifference in the direction of the everlasting No." If we cannot get certainty, we may at least find rest; and we shall be more likely to find it in works of mercy than in study, in imitating Christ rather than in arguing about Him. In most things we act upon probabilities rather than upon absolute certainty. In most things we trust our heart and instincts as much as, or more than, our intellect. In all things we depend very much upon the authority and testimony of others. Saints and martyrs and Christ our Lord lived for mankind, and died to testify to the truth of our religion; anti-Christianity cannot produce such evidence in its favour; it can only destroy; it has no man-loving, self-sacrificing saints to show, and no martyrs.

Monday after the Second Sunday.

SINS OF OMISSION.

In all our Lord's parables of the Judgment Day it is omissions of duty that are condemned and punished. In the Pounds, the Talents, the Sheep and Goats, the Virgins, the Rich Man and Lazarus, all of which lift the veil that hides the unseen world and foretell the circumstances of the last Great Assize, in all these the condemned are those who have left undone what they ought to have done. No positive actual sin is alleged against them, only they have neglected opportunities, lost time, wasted that which was entrusted to them, not been active and useful in life, done no good to their fellow-men, had no regard for the interest of God's work in the world. They are not accused of great crimes against God or man; it is idleness, thoughtlessness, uselessness with which they are charged and for which they are condemned.

Now is not this a frightening aspect of that which is before us? There are plenty of solemn warnings in Scripture that strike home upon the conscience of the transgressor of the ten commandments; but there are many who feel guiltless of open sin. Their education, the fear of man, barriers raised around them by society or by their position, these render it difficult for them to go very far astray; it is actually easier for them, up to a certain point, to do right than to do wrong. There arises involuntarily the Pharisee's self-congratulation in their hearts; they walk on high, and look down on poor grovelling sinners, and feel positively spotless by comparison with them. Yet here in our Bibles it stands, as plainly as it can be written, that we respectable, moral people, shall be hereafter examined by the Great God, not only as to the evil we have done, but as to the good we have not done.

> "Heaven does with us as we with torches do,
> Not light them for themselves. For if our virtues
> Did not go forth of us, 'twere all alike
> As if we had them not."

If the clergy talk to dying people about the necessity of turning with all the heart to God and seeking His pardon before it is too late, one of the most common answers is, "Well, I don't know that I have ever done any harm; I have not lived a bad life." Sometimes these very persons have actually done very bad things, but their poor uneducated dull consciences have a miserably low standard, and call sins by other and pleasanter names. But even if this is not the case, there is still God's judgment of the life as regards omissions, and that many never seem to think of at all. It will be seen plainly enough on the Great Day of light. When those who, like us, have received the Pound from God, come in with five Pounds or ten Pounds, and we have nothing to show but just what we originally received, the comparison will bring us down from our high place of self-satisfaction. The man in our Lord's parable had not lost his Pound; there it was; he had not spent it upon himself, and so robbed his master; he had not got into debt like the unjust Steward, or made away with everything in riotous living like the Prodigal, nor broken out into open rebellion like the Citizens; and yet his master meets him with the terrible words, "Thou wicked servant," and bids his guards take away from him his Pound, and leave him penniless as well as disgraced.

Is it not necessary for us to think of all this? Does not the Church give us Advent that we may recall these plain, awful, but forgotten truths? Is it wise to desire only to hear smooth pleasant things, when these solemn warnings were spoken by our Lord Himself, and handed down to us by the Evangelists? When the Great Day comes, and it is too late to alter mistakes, to repair omissions, to use lost opportunities; when it is impossible to begin life over again, shall we not bitterly repent our carelessness, and wildly reproach our ministers, if our thoughts have never been turned to the method of God's judgment of our life, which He has taken such pains to reveal to us by His Son?

The key to the whole matter is found in the fact that each one of us has a Master; that our life, with all its circumstances and all its possibilities, is His. People say, "May I not do what I like with my time, my money, my thoughts, my life itself?" and the New Testament answer is, "Certainly not; none of these are your own; they are God's; and He has entrusted them to you for a time, and will demand an account of their use." Are there not many lives that seem even to our eyes useless, profitless to God or man? People who saunter through life, doing nothing, caring about nothing except themselves, interested in nothing except some fancy pursuit or the day's passing trifles; who, if they take up any duty, speedily give it up; who have no time to work for God or for others, no money to give away; who make no friends, and whom few or no one will miss when they die? They have "talents" (the word taken from the Parable, originating with the popular knowledge of this English Bible of ours), but their "talents" are lost, not used, not developed. When we see the vast wealth of this great country, when we think of the leisure of so many, and then see how all good works are languishing, and that those who start them and try to carry them on are wearied and sick at heart because they are not helped, are we not sadly sure that there must be many indeed who keep their Pound laid up in a Napkin? A vast proportion of the evils of the world and of our own country are curable; the method of their cure is known, the agencies are in existence, but the drones in the human hive are many, and the work is not done.

Then, besides those who do nothing, there are those who do not as much as they might do, and those who are busy enough, but do but little good. Progress, improvement, revival, reformation, these are invariable features of the manly Christian life. All sorts of excuses are found for making a new beginning by the truly wise man. Now it is Advent; presently it will be the New-Year; then there will come Lent; then some anniversary; there is always some good reason for turning over a new leaf, reviewing the position, and seeing how it may be made better.

There is seemingly significance in the word used by our Lord, the "Napkin" in which the wasted Pound is laid up. It is in the original the handkerchief with which a man wipes away the sweat of his brow that comes through hard work. Instead of being used for this honest purpose, it is put away, and the Pound is put away with it. The word, too, is the same as is used of the dead Lazarus, "His face bound about with a Napkin." The Pound is treated like a corpse, instead of being brought out into the busy world to pass from hand to hand. So in the parable of the Talents the idle servant is said to bury his talent in the earth; the same idea; death, burial, decay, where there should be activity and increase. The man may say, "Here is thy Pound;" but it will be tarnished, perhaps corroded out of all shape and beauty, by lying unused, whereas the coin that has circulated is bright. Brain and muscle, because they are used, develop and grow, and the limb that is never exercised wastes. So with a man's life; work begets work. While the barren tree is cut down, the fruitful tree is pruned and digged about, and it grows and bears more fruit.

There is yet one more point in this parable that is worthy of attention. The faithful and diligent servants find no fault with their master, but the idle man calls him hard and austere, and fears him. As soon as Adam was convicted of his fault, he began to blame God. It is an instinct of guilt to try and clear itself at some one else's expense. True penitence cries, "My fault, my own most grievous fault," and sets about amendment. Hard thoughts of God's providence, excuses for self, envy of others, postponement of acknowledged duty, these all leave the Pound still idle in the Napkin. Conviction of fault sends the man to fetch it, and use it; thanking God for His warning and His patience. Let this be our Advent lesson to-day, and if any of us have been unprofitable servants, thank God, there is yet time to amend before the Lord comes to reckon with us.

Tuesday after the Second Sunday.

THE METHOD OF GOD'S JUDGMENT.

THERE is an evident similarity between the Song of Hannah and the Song of the Blessed Virgin, which is commonly called the Magnificat. In both there is the assertion of the overruling providence of God, His exaltation of the poor and humble, His judgment according to right. Both are thanksgivings for unexpected mercies; both celebrate the birth of a Son, granted beyond human hope, and as a Saviour from misery to His people; both contain many anticipations of the truths revealed by the Gospel of Christ. In the Song of Hannah, the special instance of God's interference on behalf of the faithful but unhappy, His reversing of man's judgment and of all human expectation, and bringing about the triumph of innocence and prayerful patience, lead on insensibly to Evangelical statements of the ultimate judgment of God, and His calling all men to account for their works by His Anointed, the Son of Man. Viewed under the influence of Gospel light and knowledge, the drift and inner meaning of the whole hymn seems to be an expansion of and comment on the words, "The Lord is a God of knowledge, and by Him actions are weighed."

Of this truth man has never altogether lost sight. The doctrines of a future life, and of a judgment according to the works done in this life, have to a great extent held their own in the minds of heathens, when so much else has been lost of God's original revelation. Thus it was that when St. Paul "reasoned of judgment to come," Felix trembled. He believed, but he had ever tried to stifle his belief in the unwelcome truth, and had so far succeeded that the awakening words of the Apostle were intolerably painful, as they made him turn his eyes where they least liked to gaze, on the terrible absence of "temperance and righteousness," till he felt sure that for him the "judgment to come" would bring condemnation. At Athens, too, while St. Paul quotes Greek poets in support of his argument against idolatry, he does not fail also to speak of the certainty of judgment to come, which was a part of the popular religion. And to go still further back, we find that the first message of the Baptist related also to this great article of faith, the coming of the Judge of all men, and the rewarding of every man according to his work.

But alas, it is not among Jews and heathens only that this truth, once known, is forgotten, or while tacitly acknowledged has lost influence and practical and energetic power over the thoughts and lives of men. We Christians have an article in our Creed, daily recited, wherein we affirm our belief that Christ shall "come again to judge the quick and the dead." Such is our professed belief, yet have we not need, even the best of us, to be ever and anon "put in mind of these things, though we know them?" Have we not need to be reminded, not only of the fact of the Judgment to come, but of the nature of that Judgment, and of the attributes and qualities of the Judge?

It is a deep and wide, as well as an awful subject; we cannot attempt to embrace the whole; let us take then those two points only which these words of Hannah's song bring before us, the knowledge of the Judge, how, why, and to what extent He knows us and our doings, and His method of passing sentence upon our lives by "weighing" our actions.

We know who will be our Judge, not the eternal Father, not the eternal Spirit, but the Son of God, who is also "Son of Man;" to Him the Father "hath committed all judgment;" to Him in deepest love, because He would not condemn any creature whom His fiat had called into being; to Him in strictest justice, for though the Father knows the secrets of all hearts, yet it is not in the same way as the Son of Man knows them, by actual human life, temptation, and suffering. Here then is our Judge; He who is a "God of knowledge," knowing what is in man, not only by being his Maker, not only by His divine Omniscience, but above all by personal experimental knowledge, as Man Himself, one of us; Man now, Man ever. Therefore we pray, "by Thy holy Incarnation, by Thy holy Nativity and Circumcision, by Thy Baptism, Fasting and Temptation, by Thy precious Death and Burial, Good Lord deliver us;" and that too, not only "in all time of our tribulation, and in all time of our wealth," *i.e.*, in this life, in its two conditions of prosperity and adversity, but also "in the hour of death, and in the day of Judgment."

> "Thou our throbbing flesh hast worn,
> Thou our mortal griefs hast borne,
> Thou hast shed the human tear,
> Jesus, Son of Mary, hear.
>
> Thou hast bowed the dying Head,
> Thou Thine own life's Blood hast shed,
> Thou hast lain in mortal bier,
> Jesus, Son of Mary, hear."

We think of the human knowledge of Jesus now when

we pray to Him in sorrow, in penitence, in love, let us not forget that He will still have that same knowledge of our inner selves when He sits upon the great white Throne, and our eyes look upon His human Face, and we hear all the past recalled, and every secret thing revealed, and viewed according to the view of a Man. For though He is very God, yet He is also very Man, and "as face answereth to face, so the heart of man to man." For this reason it is perhaps that "books" are mentioned at the Judgment. Were the Eternal Father the Judge, such mundane and human accessories would be out of place, but the Judge is "Son of Man;" any detail that will remind us of this is important, and its mention is not unmeaning. As all power is of God, and all human power points to, and is a faint semblance of the ruling power of the Supreme and Almighty God, so all human judgment, all tribunals, all punishments, set forth as in parable the last Great Assize, when the just Man, the holy and perfect Man, shall sit as Judge, and His fellow-men shall be tried by Him, and acknowledge not only His authority and His justice, but His "knowledge" of them and of their actions.

Such then is the Judge. Now see how He administers His office, how He uses His "knowledge." "By Him actions are weighed." Let us notice that word, and mark its force and significance. Weighing is an act of comparison; we compare what we weigh with some standard which we place in the opposite scale. But God knows all things; He has no need of this comparison; it is for our sake then that actions are weighed, that we and all mankind may see by the evidence of our own senses what is our true condition, and acknowledge the justice of the irreversible sentence of the Judge. "All the ways of a man are clean in his own eyes, but God weigheth the spirits." God sees the end from the beginning; He is the great "I am;" He knows who are His, but He will prove His justice to our senses and our reason, that all flesh may be silent before Him, every mouth stopped, every mind convinced of His mercy and truth, those whom He acquits and those whom He condemns alike.

What then will be the standard by which He will try us and our actions? By what shall we be "weighed" in the balance of the sanctuary? First and chiefly by the one standard of perfect manhood, the Man Christ Jesus. His life is now our pattern and model, it will then be the standard by which we shall be tried. He was man, He was in all points tempted like as we are. It may not be that heathen and Jew will be tried by this high and perfect standard, it seems more reasonable that they should not. For the one there would seem to be the law of conscience, for the other the law of Moses; but for us Christians what criterion can there be but the perfect revelation of God's will respecting man in the life of Christ; the Man in whom God was well pleased?

Are we prepared for this? By Him our actions shall be "weighed;" our obedience by His obedience; our regard for the will of God by His; our love and mercy to our fellow-men by His; our prayers, our daily walk, our whole life, our secret selves, our dearest aims, all weighed against His. Let us thus look at our lives, and where is there room for pride and vainglory? Let us look thus at our good works, our alms deeds, our good dispositions, the best and choicest that we have to show, in which we ourselves sometimes rejoice, and which others praise and envy in us; and what shall we say? God's word puts the right answer into our mouths, "O Lord, if Thou art extreme to mark what is done amiss, who may abide it? All our righteousness is as filthy rags; enter not into judgment with Thy servant, O Lord, for in Thy sight shall no man living be justified. Mine eye seeth Thee, wherefore I abhor myself, and repent in dust and ashes."

Yes, this is the right answer; this the right result of judging ourselves now, that we may not be judged and condemned hereafter, "I abhor myself;" for the beginning of true wisdom is humility; "I repent;" for it is written, "Except ye repent, ye shall perish." This is our wisdom, our safety, our hope, to repent; and again and again to repent; to repent of past repentances; to confess our sins that they may be forgiven, washed away, annihilated, that in that day they may not be found, and we may stand justified before the Judge of truth and righteousness, relying not only upon His mercy, but upon His justice to acquit us, saying with Job's confidence, "Let me be weighed in an even balance, that God may know my integrity."

But there will be another standard by which our actions will be "weighed." These very repentances, and the works meet for repentance, and all else that concerns our sins, and our recovery from them, there can be no comparison of these with the Man Christ Jesus, for He was without sin. He was the Just One Who needed no repentance. How then will the Judge weigh these our acts of repentance, of reparation, of returning to God? Holy Scripture will tell us this also. Do we not read of the Apostles "sitting on twelve thrones," united with Christ in His judgment; and of the "saints judging the world?" They were not perfect like their Lord; they needed repentance, and they did repent to salvation. By their true repentances then, perhaps, will our repentances be weighed. And wherever else the standard of the Son of Man is above us, there His "saints shall judge the world," men and women of like passions with ourselves, who like us have been weak, and who out of weakness have been made strong; who like us have been tempted, and who have "overcome by the Blood of the Lamb;" who like us have sinned, and who have repented and been pardoned. By their actions, our actions will be "weighed;" for as they were, so are we in the world. God is not unrighteous; what He did for them, He will do for us also if we will.

This truth seems to be taught in several of our Lord's parables, which evidently point out the method of the last Judgment. Thus the five foolish Virgins are condemned by the opposite conduct of the five wise. The idle Servants who received the pound and the talent, are seen to be without excuse when their more diligent brethren display the results of their life-work. Those who have neglected to minister to the wants of their fellow-men, go away silent and convicted, when they see how others, in exactly the same circumstances, have performed a worthier part, and so ministered unawares to Christ Himself.

Nor is this all. If we fail to correspond to this standard, there is yet another and a lower standard by which we shall be "weighed," that we and all the world may acknowledge the justice of the shameful and hopeless doom of the unworthy Christian. Our Lord Himself says, "The men of Nineveh shall rise in the Judgment with this generation, and shall condemn it; the Queen of the South shall rise up in the Judgment with this generation, and shall condemn it." The one repented at the preaching of judgment, the other was attracted by the love of wisdom. "This generation," the generation to whom Christ is preached, is continually invited to repentance, continually has the offer of wisdom; if we repent not, if we become not "wise unto salvation," shall we not be weighed in the balances with these pre-Christian worthies, and being found wanting, shall be justly condemned to everlasting shame and contempt.

Such then will be the great Judgment. Thus will our "actions be weighed" by the standard of Christ, of His saints, and of the worthy heathen. And more than this; surely each action will itself be weighed, with all its circumstances, its special guilt or merit, its aggravations or extenuations; for sins are evidently of different degrees, some greater, some less than others. The same sin is more exceeding sinful in one man than in another; the same good deed is more meritorious in one man than in another. We know this; but we know too that human law and justice cannot take cognisance of these fine but important distinctions; we cannot "weigh" men's actions, just because we have not sufficient "knowledge" of all the remote and proximate influences that surround and affect them. Human justice is clumsy, inflexible; it works like a machine, only in one uniform routine. Not so the Justice of God, for "the Lord is a God of knowledge, by Him actions are weighed." Hence it shall be that the Judgment shall bring about such vast changes, so that "the last shall be first, and the first last." We scarcely know what we ourselves are, or what we shall be, for the heart is deceitful; therefore we do not venture to commend ourselves, or to judge ourselves, but leave all to Him who judgeth righteously.

This then is He with whom we have to do, the Righteous Judge, "who will render to every man according to his works; to them who by patient continuance in well-doing, seek for glory and honour and immortality, eternal life; but unto them that obey not the truth, but obey unrighteousness, indignation and wrath, tribulation and anguish, upon every soul of man that doeth evil; but glory, honour, and peace, to every one that worketh good; in the day when God shall judge the secrets of man by Jesus Christ."

Wednesday after the Second Sunday.

BLESSED PURITY.

A MODERN writer has said in disparagement of Christianity, that "Innocence rather than nobility is its ideal." Innocence is the ideal of Christianity, but it does not therefore follow that it cannot produce true nobility. A fallen angel, such as some of our great poets or painters have pictured, whether truly or not, is a creature grand and terrible, but the angel that has kept his first estate is after all more noble. The man who falls, and errs, and struggles with but poor success in the battle of life and in the contest between good and evil, may be great and picturesque, but the man who stands firm in his integrity from youth to age is really more noble, and fulfils God's intention in his creation better. The heathen knew nothing of purity. To the philosopher it was an impossible dream; to the world at large it was unknown or unvalued. Christianity is like no other religious system, it does not deal with the mature man only, but begins its work upon the unconscious infant; it forestalls evil by good. The guilt of Original Sin is attacked by Baptism, and the babe is made pure; and then the whole Christian system is contrived to keep up that purity to the end of life. There is a whole system indeed and a complete apparatus for the pardon of sin, for the restoration of the fallen, but the primary idea of Christianity is purity; and it is only when this has been lost that the secondary idea, renovation, comes into sight.

This is often forgotten, and so Christian children are left alone, as if they had as yet nothing to do with Christ and His religion, or they are tormented with entreaties to seek for a sense of sin and a desire for conversion, which is altogether unreal to them and unnatural, because in point of fact they do not need it; their sins are few, their faults not deliberate transgressions against knowledge and conviction, but infirmities that scarcely sully their baptismal purity. These are the "ninety-nine just persons that need no repentance;" these are they "whose angels ever behold the face of God." Children will be far greater in number in heaven than adults.

The whole system of religion with many is summed up in one word, Conversion, a change of heart. They have no place for the pure in heart. A man must be a great sinner, or they do not know what to do with him. What wonder then that they cannot understand Christ's sacraments, that they think lightly of the Baptism of infants, that their highest ideal of a Christian is a reclaimed drunkard or profligate, that instead of taking Christ's word, "blessed are the pure in heart," they have invented a new motto, "The greater the sinner, the greater the saint?" But, thank God, this is not Christianity. Christ Himself is our model, the pure, the Blessed One. The little child was His ideal and example; and then, if that failed, if purity was lost, if the child became a Peter or a Magdalen, then there was a door of hope, a way of penitence and restoration.

Let none prefer penitence to purity. As well might we prefer the mended vase to the new one without flaw or crack; as well cut off our sound limbs that we might adopt some clever artificial substitute. God's intention for man, as for the angels, was purity. The highest places in heaven are for the pure in heart, not for the penitent, however great and glorious. St. John tells us how these virgin souls follow the Lamb whithersoever He goeth; they enter a circle of familiarity that the fallen may never pass; and David tells us in the Psalms of these same virgins that accompany the Bride, and enter into the King's palace; they "See God;" that is, they possess Him, and are possessed by Him in mutual love, for such is the force of the phrase, just as we read, "See corruption," "See the Kingdom of God," "See life."

Purity once lost is like water spilt upon the ground; it can never be regained. It is a delicate flower, which if once sullied or faded, no power can restore again to its original perfection. This gives the key-note to true Christian education. "Now thou art clean, keep thyself pure." The child is taught to honour, reverence, and glory in his purity, to guard it as a precious treasure of God which the world, for very love of mischief and destruction, applies all its energies to rob him of, that it may trample it under foot. Christ gives him aids, armour and arms, to protect his purity, strength by sacraments to overcome temptation, and to carry this fragile, beautiful thing through this rude, rough world, safe to the place whence it came, and where it will flourish as in its native climate.

We forget all this very often. We look out into the world, and see sin and vileness rampant; every degree of defilement and degradation of God's work, and we get to take it as a matter of course, and at best hope for an amendment some day, as if this were the ordinary rule, and nothing better were possible, or had been designed by God, and made ours by Christ. Christ and the New

Testament are against us if we think so; the records of God's saints, little known now, will in the day of light and revelation be opened to condemn us. Men and women and children we shall then see who have lived in this world, where we have fallen, ever pure in heart; pure *in heart*, no whited sepulchres, fair and comely outside, and within full of corruption and rottenness, but glorious Temples of God saturated with His presence in every part, whose eyes, not blurred and blinded by sin, have seen God, when others groped in darkness and knew Him not, though He was not far from any one of them; who have seen God and been guided by His eye; who have seen Him in His word, in His works, in His sacraments, in His providence; whose hearts, not perverted by the world, have, by intuition, perceived dangers and avoided them, into which others have stupidly walked; whose souls, bright and quick, have been alive to the world unseen, and have held almost constant intercourse, even here, with its persons and things; whose minds have had no difficulties with hard questions, but have rested calmly upon faith. These were no weak, insensible, passionless beings, but rather men and women, who, with great capabilities for good or for evil, have boldly, finally, chosen good; who with strong passions, and eager, impetuous desires have yet kept all in subjection, and directed their natural energies into unpolluting avocations, and whose happy dreams have not been haunted by the ever-reviving memories of past sins, which come unbidden, endued with hateful, quenchless vitality, to torment those who have once made themselves familiar with that which defileth; who have ever gone on and grown in grace, with scarce a fall, scarce a drawback, fulfilling the end of their creation, till they have passed away to see God indeed, in the happy brightness of His Kingdom.

To many all this is unreal; they have never heard of such persons, much less seen them. The people they meet day by day are quite different; they are quite different themselves. They have never read the lives of those who have lived by a higher rule, who have taken Christ at His word, and really followed Him. Let such remember that as there are higher paths of knowledge, of science, of skill, which are beyond them, yet are well known to some, so is it with the religion of Christ. We know in our own hearts that if we had kept ourselves pure we might have been greater, higher far than we are or ever can be now; and there have been and are those who have done this, and have become greater than we could ever have been. Who can tell how hard and unnatural we have made Christ's service by our own Esau-like bartering of our original purity for some momentary sin? How much of our unsatisfactory spiritual state may be explained by this, that we are still climbing up the narrow, steep by-path of repentance when we might have been walking upon the straight, plain way of purity, in the footsteps of Christ; that we cannot see, because we have laden ourselves with thick clay; that there is dimness, and weakness, and pain, and want of joyous zest because we are diseased and lamed, because by the loss of purity we have lost the freshness of perpetual youth, that runs and is not weary, that walks and is not faint, and are prematurely old, and worn, and broken. Why are women more religious than men, but because they are purer? Why can some walk unscathed through temptations, and undergo trials and afflictions that crush and ruin others, but because they are purer? " To him that hath shall more be given." The fire discovers the pure metal. The flaw in the work is soon seen when sufficient pressure is applied; the sound constitution stands, while those who have hidden weaknesses one after another break down under long privation and hardships. Just so the pure in heart are strong. The old Christian poets loved to sing of fire that could not burn them, of wild beasts that licked their feet and did their bidding, of wilder men that were subdued by God's own purity that gleamed softly from their virgin eyes, and mastered all by its gentle omnipotence.

But with all this let us not forget that the converse of Christ's Beatitude is dreadfully true, "Cursed are the impure, for they shall not see God." All God's revelation teaches this, the Jewish washings, the words of Christ, the teaching of prophets and seers. Nothing that defileth, or is defiled, can enter the holy place, only the pure in heart, and the cleansed and pardoned penitent. Time would fail did we attempt to bring together the proofs of this in the words, the parables, the revelations of scripture. And why need we do so when few doubt it? Why need we do so when the impure know that their chief desire is secrecy; when we know that sin hides itself invariably from the eyes of man and from God? "See God!" nay, anything but that! The great hope and reward of the pure is the one terror of the impure. The pure are naked, yet not ashamed; the impure are clothed, yet they try to hide themselves further and further, deeper and deeper, from the eye of God. There is a mutual revulsion. The impure say to God, "Depart from us;" and God will say to the impure hereafter, "Depart from Me."

But, thank God, there is a middle course between these two, between this way of destruction, and that way of purity. The way that is strewn with crosses, and thorns, and stumbling blocks, that is haunted by evil ones, that is full of pitfalls and dark places, and bye-paths that lead all wrong; yet for all but the pure it is the only way of hope, the only way that leads to heaven, the only way now for them unless they turn back to perdition. The father's chief blessing is for the son who never transgressed his commandment, never forsook his home, the faithful supplanter Jacob; but even for the prodigal, even for the shameful, wasteful Esau, in Christ there is yet a blessing, and there is joy among the angels of God over the sinner that repenteth.

But, oh, happy those young unstained souls to whom the highest paths of glory are yet open, which to penitents are for ever closed! Happy they on whose heads that special circlet of pure gold may yet glitter for all eternity! Happy they into whose faces Christ yet looks, and loves them, and calls them to be perfect! This world is opening upon them and smiling, and men bid them take a high place, and carve out for themselves a great future; but Christ says to them, "Look higher, aim at better than all this; there is a world waiting to be revealed of endless, sinless joys, of knowledge, and greatness, and beauty, and power, and majesty, beyond the best here, as light is beyond darkness; to you are offered there the highest places, God's chosen, reserved gifts; you He would make nobles, princes, kings, in that dazzling Kingdom; be bold, be brave, rise to the height of your great destiny, be pure in heart, so shall you ever be blessed, in the sight of men, and angels, and God."

Thursday after the Second Sunday.

THE TOUCH OF CHRIST.

THERE is something very touching in the circumstances of the miracle of the healing of the woman with an issue of blood. We cannot help sympathising with this poor afflicted woman; we think of the twelve long years of weary suffering, the oft tried remedies and physicians, the oft-raised, oft-disappointed hopes; we admire the greatness of the courage that enabled her to worm her way, poor weak invalid as she was, through that thronging crowd, in which mere pushing vulgar curiosity must have formed so large an element; we respect the shrinking womanly modesty that made her hide her infirmity, and steal up unseen by all to touch her Lord; nay, not Him, but His garment, and that but the utmost hem. We all know something of sickness and bodily afflictions, they call out our best and tenderest feelings, we melt with gentleness towards the suffering; and so when our Lord, for His own wise reasons and great purposes, will have this poor thing out before all; when He will not allow her to steal away as she came; when His word draws her blushing, trembling, weeping, out into the midst of that circle of eyes; and when she falls upon her knees, and hides her shame-mantled face with her poor thin quivering hands, and sobs out all the tale of her secret sorrow; we feel almost indignant with our Lord, as if He were inconsiderate, ungentle, not Himself, that He should thus lacerate so tender a nature.

But it is not with these thoughts that we would occupy our minds just now. There is much else that this miracle teaches, but there is one wonderful truth, old as creation, wide as the animated world, the very core and marrow of Christianity which is brought out in this incident, which may well claim our attention, which it behoves us to know well, to remember always, to be reminded of ever and again. Our Lord specially commends the wisdom and faith of this woman which taught her to say to herself, "If I may but touch His garment I shall be whole." And why? Because she was uttering a great and eternal truth; because she had discovered a radical and essential principle in the economy of God. Let her be our teacher; let us learn her lesson that we too may be healed and blessed.

Where shall we begin to explain in fewest words so great and wide and essential a truth? Take we the word picture itself as we have set it up before our mind's eye. The pale, wasted, dying woman touches the garment of Jesus, and in a moment she is well. The obstinate disease is gone; the inward long aggravated mischief is repaired; the shadow of death that was stealing over that poor body, soon to take possession of it, and bring it to destruction, is chased away, and life, warm, vigorous, joyous life, reigns instead. How is this? Let us approach step by step to the answer. See yonder lamp flickering, its flame dim, smaller and smaller, dull red, choked with its own ashes; now see one pour oil into the lamp, and what a change! The flame rises, clears, brightens, burns away all that would keep it down, and sheds light around. See the bare ground, the dry dead trees upon which snow and wind and cold have beaten all the winter months, and come some warm, genial Spring morning, when the soft shower has been stealing down all night, and see the tender green shoots coming up from the fragrant ground, and the buds swelling upon tree and shrub almost before our eyes. See the sick child upon whom the healing specific begins to operate; watch eye and pulse and cheek; what a wondrous change is going on. Look at the poor starved frame that has been recovered from the sea or the mine; friction and warmth and nourishment are working wonders upon it every moment; there is something stirring in every limb, every part and function, and getting possession of all.

What is it that is going on in all these cases? It is the struggle between two great principles, preservation and destruction, death and life. We have no idea what life is. Vegetable, animal, human life, one and all are beyond our powers of investigation; we get up to a certain point, and there we are baffled; what we search for always eludes us; we cannot hold it; we cannot find out whence it comes, how it exists, why it departs. It is not likely we shall ever find it out. It seems to be part of the mystery of God. He is the Author of life, and He who came into the world in human flesh declares Himself to be "The Life," the Source and Spring of all life.

And now notice the law of life, which He the Creator ordained in this world of ours. The first forms of life in the world were vegetable forms; the life began in some obscure manner; it had the power of taking up from earth and air what it needed to sustain and develop itself. Then the powers of life languished and failed, and death set in, and then came destruction. Next this world saw the animal creation, higher forms of life endued with powers of motion and many other attributes which were unknown in the world of vegetable life.

But still the same laws held good; life was mysteriously propagated; it appropriated what it needed; it renewed itself, and flourished for a time, and then the law of death set in, and the end came. But then came the Creation of man, not a mere animal, but with wonderful God-like powers of mind and soul. Shall he too die? No, his pure vitality renews itself ever; waste is always restored; life is always dominant. Within his reach there is set up the Tree of Life. This is the food of immortality, the medicine to counteract the tendency to decay, the food to sustain life always. He eats and lives for ever. But man falls, and death is the punishment of sin. The Tree of Life is cut off; the ills of the flesh can no more be healed absolutely; the powers of destruction work on gradually but surely to the end. "As soon as we are born, we begin to die;" the struggle between life and death goes on for a while, in some a longer time, in some a shorter time; life renews itself and exists for a certain period; but death is steadily making its approaches; it is felt now here, now there; life retires step by step, till death is master everywhere, and the man is dead.

But now there comes into the world the second Adam, the author and Creator of all things, Himself Life. His human frame pure, His soul sinless, death has no dominion over Him, sickness and disease cannot touch Him; nay, there goes virtue out of Him; life streams from Him; His touch chases away disease and death; the Tree of Life is restored to earth. And even when He went away His wondrous power was not withdrawn; He left it to His Apostles; the touch of their hands, the power of their intercession, even the contact of their bodies, their shadow, their clothes, were the channels of life to death-threatened bodies.

But the mission of Christ was not so much to bring life to dying bodies, as to dead souls. He Himself laid down His life, He submitted to death in the body, and He did not see fit to exempt us from it; but the second death, the death of the soul, this He was careful to conquer thoroughly, and to make us partakers of His victory. It is in Him alone that there is life; to lay hold on Him is the only way to escape death. "If I may but touch Him, I shall be whole." Man cannot see God, much less touch Him, but God clothed Himself in human flesh; this is the garment that we may touch. When He went away in the flesh, He remained in the world in sacrament and spiritual presence; "lo, I am with you alway, even to the end of the world." The sacraments are the continuation of the Incarnation. The Holy Ghost abides ever in the Church, "the Author and Giver of life;" by Him we may touch Christ ever and be healed; by Him sin is pardoned, the soul is fed, the spiritual life is sustained and developed. Christ is never absent; He is within the reach of all; the Tree of Life is open to all; Christ is multiplied in His appointed ministers; "as my Father sent Me, so send I you; and lo, I am with you alway." They have received freely, and they freely give the treasures of life which Christ brought from Heaven. Christ is in our midst; He is thronged and pressed upon by the seething multitude; but, alas! there is wanting in many the faith that can appropriate the virtue that ever flows out from Him. Some are ignorant; some misled, mistaught; and while they fancy they honour Christ, they wound Him, and injure themselves. Many are busy with this dying world, and have no care for the life that ends not. Those only are blessed who follow the example of this poor woman;

whose faith has been educated to say, "If I may but touch Him, I shall be whole;" and whom nothing can keep back from Him; who with violence lay hold on eternal life. Let this poor woman, then, be our teacher. Death is around us, within us; it is stealing over our bodies, and soon it will make them its prey; let us leave our garment in its hand, and flee; let us lay hold on eternal life, that death may have no dominion over us, in our very selves, the immaterial soul. There is no life but in God, its Author and Source; there is no way to Him but by the Man Christ Jesus; and He is not far from any one of us. Wherever His Church and sacraments and ministry are, there are still the skirts of His clothing. Never mind the throng of unwise; be our place with this faithful daughter of Abraham; let us believe, hope, draw near, touch; so shall we too be healed.

Friday after the Second Sunday.

THE WICKEDNESS OF THE UNLOVING HEART.

THERE is much Advent instruction in the parable of the Unmerciful Servant, too much to be fully entered upon at one time. There are some obvious and plain lessons; there is an application that can scarcely be missed, that lies upon the surface, and hardly needs that any one should point it out; and there are also other less prominent teachings, not less important because probably often overlooked.

The parable tells us of the servant of a great king who owes a vast sum to his lord; he is utterly unable to pay; he is condemned to suffer the penalty of his defalcations. Then he throws himself wholly upon the gratuitous compassion of the king; and not only is his punishment remitted, but the vast hopeless debt itself is cancelled; a boon he never asked for, nor even thought of. But no sooner has he recovered from the shock of so great a joy, than he plays the tyrant to one of his fellow-servants who happens to be in his power. The king hears of his cruelty, calls for him, and addresses him, "O thou wicked servant;" and at once rescinds his pardon, and lays the suspended punishment upon him.

Now let us examine this exclamation and epithet of the king. The king in the greatness of his magnanimity takes the man's profession as true and heartfelt; he believes that it has been through misfortune, and not by any dishonesty or wickedness, that the enormous debt has been incurred; he pities the abject condition of his subordinate; he not only pardons him, but with princely reckless liberality makes him a present of the immense sum that he owed to the treasury. But this deed of hard grasping cruelty, done too at such a time and under such aggravating circumstances, convinces the king that he has been deceived; that the man is unworthy of his mercy and his generosity; that he is bad at heart; that he is a thief and an impostor. His eyes are opened. He that is unjust in this least matter, has doubtless been unjust in the great matter; he who could perpetrate such a crime against mercy, even when the heavenly streams of mercy were actually pouring down upon him from head to foot, could also have wilfully robbed his lord to this vast amount. He who could rob at such a rate could play a part of innocence. The king sees it all; the mask has fallen off; the man himself has lifted just a corner of the thick veil that hides his black heart, and has shown himself a monster unfit to be loose among his fellow-men; for their sake, and for the sake of all that is good and true, he is removed to a fitting place and a safe distance. The epithet then seems to be emphatic, "O thou *wicked* servant!" His master had thought him honourable, but unfortunate; perhaps inefficient, but certainly not criminal. Now he sees what he is, and with surprise and indignation calls him what he sees he is, "wicked."

Such then appears to be the force of this part of the parable, taken by itself as a separate study. But when we come to apply it to our own instruction, a difficulty at once suggests itself. If, as our Lord explains, the king is the type of the great Father and Judge, and if this wicked servant is the impenitent sinner, how can there be any force in that which we have made the point of the

THE UNLOVING HEART. 87

whole incident, the king's finding out the man's unworthiness by the accidental revelation of his minor crime? To God all is known, nothing is accidental; no finding out is possible with respect to Him; none need tell Him, for He knows all things; all is naked and open to Him always. All this is true, and the same or some similar difficulty may be found in all parables, analogies, symbols, and types. They all fail somewhere. Nature cannot perfectly reveal that which is above nature. There is likeness, not identity; there is general similarity, a similarity in some special characteristics, but difference, contrast, even opposition elsewhere. God indeed cannot be said to "find us out," but He may wish us to find out ourselves, and He may give us opportunities of doing so, when we are following a deceitful path, taking in our fellow-men, blinding even our own selves.

There is indeed a vast debt of sin and trespass which we owe to God, but it has stood so long, He has so overlooked it, He has seemingly pardoned it, that it gives us no uneasiness; we think that we are safe, that we may do what we will because God is so merciful, that we shall escape condemnation at the last great scrutiny. Now what does God in His goodness do for us, when we thus blind ourselves to the whole truth of His revelation of Himself and His will? He will give us an opportunity of seeing ourselves as we are, by some little matter between man and man. A straw will tell the way of the wind; little things, little actions, passing words, looks, and thoughts, tell us what we are in the inner man, which is our real self, and which will last when all external things have passed away. We are off our guard in little things; in great matters we take care to put on the mask, to assume the stage dress and gait; we are natural in passing trifles. By these small things then we are taught to judge ourselves; for, alas, we go on year after year, some of us, and are ignorant of our real selves. If a man goes away and forgets his own face that he has just seen in the glass, how easily may we be ignorant what manner of men we are in our inmost hearts, which we have so many inducements carefully to conceal. We may be kept from great sins by other restraints than those of true religion; we must see therefore whether the sins themselves are cherished and loved secretly, by noticing whether their more mild forms are allowed and indulged in. We may be afraid of the world and of present consequences, and so keep from gross sins; but what is the real state of our hearts? How do we think of certain sins when we are not likely to be found out, or to suffer for them? Do not some of us really love this or that sin far more than God, and should we not indulge in it far more than we do, if we did not fear, not God, but the world? There is many a one who deserves the name of "wicked," who is highly esteemed among men; but God looks at the heart, and sees sin dwelling there, enthroned as king, loved, obeyed, beyond all else. The aim and purpose of Christianity is to renew, to regenerate us, to make us like God; and its work begins within; the cup and platter are first cleansed within; if that has not yet been done, nothing has been done. Let us recollect that we are not saved in our sins, but from our sins, by Christ. All outward decency, all external obedience and conformity to ordinances and observances, is empty, useless, deceitful, if within us all the while the heart is "wicked."

It is important for us to notice the special way in which the parable bids us test the real state of our hearts.

It is hard to say whether we love God. God is so great, so incomprehensible, so unknown; how shall we find out the state of our heart towards Him? How shall we know whether we are going the way that will lead us to Him? The parable answers these questions; and illustrates St. John's words, "If a man say, I love God, and hateth his brother, he is a liar; for he that loveth not his brother whom he hath seen, how can he love God whom he hath not seen?" God's rule is twofold; we must love God, and we must love our brother. We may test the former by the latter. If we fail in the latter, there is God's sentence hanging over us, "O thou wicked servant." If we are guilty in the matter of these hundred pence as regards our brother, we may be sure we stand indebted to God in those ten thousand talents. "By this shall it be known that ye are my disciples, if ye have love (not towards Me, but) one toward another."

Let us try ourselves by this easy test, how we act towards our fellow-men, and we shall know how we stand in relation to God. There are poor; there are charitable institutions; there are schools; there are missions; "he that seeth his brother have need, and shutteth up his compassion from him, how dwelleth the love of God in him?" Notice that the "love of God" is proved not to exist in the heart by the presence of an unloving, grudging spirit, that suffers real pain when asked to give. Let us think of our words and thoughts, of our feeling with respect to forgiveness of injuries, of our measure of kindness, of our willingness to make the best, to hope the best; let us honestly think what is our general temper and rule of conduct towards those with whom our lot is cast day by day. The tongue that smites our brother cannot rightly bless God, so says our

Lord; again the same test, the same rule. The man who injures his neighbour, qualifies himself for God's eternal verdict, "O thou wicked servant;" not wicked on this account only, but wicked previously, wicked in heart, proved so by this outward act, as the tree is known by its fruit.

Let this then be our lesson to-day. We may see how we stand with God, by noticing what manner of spirit we are of with respect to those about us. Unloving acts come from a wicked heart, a heart that is alienated from God, and only wants the removal of mere human restraints to make it break out in its real character, a heart that has no love of God in it, that could not be happy with God, that never can be with God. Let us thank God who gives such tests and such warnings, to withdraw us from evil, and keep us in the right way. They send us to our knees, saying, "Create in me a clean heart, O God;" they lay us prostrate at the foot of the Cross, saying, "Wash me again, and yet again, from mine iniquity." They are that "loving correction that maketh us great," that "fear of the Lord, which is the beginning of wisdom."

Saturday after the Second Sunday.

CHRIST'S BROTHER, SISTER, AND MOTHER.

AMONG all the words of our Blessed Lord there are none more gracious and wonderful than these, "Whosoever shall do the will of my Father which is in heaven, the same is my brother, and sister, and mother;" and not only wonderful, but most cheering and consoling to every soul that is striving to serve God, however imperfect its success may be. They must have been held to be important and memorable words, for three of the four Evangelists record them, while so many of our Lord's sacred utterances have been allowed to pass away; though doubtless these unrecorded words have not actually been lost, for they helped to mould the character of the Apostles, and through them to teach the Church that unwritten instinct that has guided her teaching in every age since Pentecost. Just as the odour hangs about the vase that has contained some precious perfume; just as the arrow speeds on with the impulse received at first from the bow; just as the man is unconsciously what he is because of training and gentle influences when he was a child, so the life and words of our Lord are still the moving power that shapes the character and inspires the soul's aspirations of Christian men and women in this nineteenth century, as they have been doing in every land and in every country where the Church has been planted.

This utterance of our Lord is one that expresses the essential and fundamental nature of His religion. It is not an unimportant branch that springs among a thousand others like it from the topmost limits of the great tree to which He likens His Kingdom, but it comes directly from the root; it is an integral portion of the main trunk, upon which all depends. It teaches us the marvellous love of God for us His creatures; it proclaims a universal brotherhood; it tells us that our Heavenly Father has adopted each one of us into His family, and that each is "*the* child of God," loved as if he alone were the object of the deep and infinite love of the eternal Father's heart.

Family ties, kinship, clan obligations, were well understood in the East. Love and duty demanded care and service within these bounds, but there was a feeling that beyond them men might be otherwise regarded and treated as enemies, or as the lawful prey of rapine and cunning. Men had no higher rule than the lower animals, who recognising a duty towards those of their own flock or herd, treat all others as intruders and objects of attack. Against this our Lord set Himself. His human heart loved His own flesh and blood, but He had room there for more than them. He took human nature in its essence; He was born without human father, and every man, woman, and child became His relation, a member of His family. "His brethren" may have been step-brothers and sisters, the children of Joseph by a former wife, or they may have been only cousins who are often called "brethren" in the Bible. Universal and unvarying tradition, and other stronger reasons, quite preclude the idea that they were the actual children of Joseph and Mary, but we cannot doubt that our Lord as a perfect Man, as an Oriental, as a son of Abraham, would have a special, real, and very powerful love for His own blood relations. If St. Paul uses such strong expressions

CHRIST'S BROTHER, SISTER, AND MOTHER. 93

of devotion to his "brethren according to the flesh," and declares his readiness to suffer and sacrifice himself for them, we may be quite certain that the pure loving heart of Jesus must have been full of tender affection to His kinsfolk, and that notwithstanding their dull inability to see His greatness, their not believing on Him, their fancy that He was " beside Himself," He would be very patient with them, and would feel Himself bound to try and win them to faith, that they might be as near to Him in His eternal Kingdom as they were in the relations of this life. What the actual record wants we may perhaps supply from the typical histories, Abraham's patient affection for Lot, Isaac's clinging to his family long unseen and unknown by face, and insisting that his son should take his wife from among them; above all the passionate love of Joseph for his brethren, in spite of their cruelty to him, and his deep yearning attachment to Benjamin his own mother's son, these and other Bible stories tell us in type and shadow the warm intuitive devotion that the Man Christ Jesus must have had for all that were His "brethren."

But there is something far beyond all this. All the world admires and wonders at the mutual love of mother and child. The mother gives her flesh and blood to form her child's body; it is not so much her own, as herself. Even the lower animals display marvellous attachment to their offspring, tenderest love, deep joy in the possession of their treasure, reckless courage in defending them, readiness to die for them or with them. And the child clings to its mother, and repays her love by responsive love. Nor does age alter this. What picture so touching, so beautiful, as a grown-up son's devotion to his mother? What love more pure, more noble, more honourable to human nature? And now let us remember what Mary was by the grace of God; let us remember what Jesus was by His own spotless nature; and then let us think, if we can, what must have been the depth, the warmth, the beauty, of the mutual love of that Mother and that Son. We must be quite certain that the world has never seen anything like it, nor ever can. And yet our Lord says that whosoever will do the will of God, the same is to Him, not only as a brother or a sister, but as His mother! There can be nothing beyond this. Words are exhausted, similes, ideas, experiences, can do no more. If such love will not win our hearts, surely nothing can touch us. Our hearts must be not flesh and blood, but stone, not human but savage beasts' hearts, or serpents' that no man can tame, charm he never so wisely.

Those "brethren" of our Lord must have constantly distressed His soul by their mundane ideas, "If Thou doest these things, show Thyself to the world." They were but narrow-minded, untaught peasants, living in a corner of the world, shut in by traditional jealousies, shut out from the thoughts and aspirations that were moving the great souls of great men in the advanced centres of civilisation. Even His mother, with all her unapproachable qualifications, must to Him, "who chargeth the angels with folly," have daily given cause for patience and pardon. And yet He loved her, loved her intensely, loved her as the great love those that are vastly inferior to them, not expecting too much, knowing exactly what they are, rejoicing in their good qualities, and not blaming them because they are not greater, because they are inferior to their own.

There is nothing so elevating to the inferior as the

condescending love of the superior. The lesser not only feels honoured and raised by the affection, but is stimulated to make itself less unworthy of the love. And so it is always improving, always gaining something, always becoming more like its nobler companion. To take an example; why has the dog ceased to be the low cowardly degraded beast that it is in the East, and become almost human in intelligence, in affection, in sympathies? Is it not simply because man has made the dog his companion and friend, and the creature has been developed, and all its good qualities have been augmented and enlarged? If an animal may thus be transformed by contact with man, what may not we become as the friends of God, the intimate relations of Jesus Christ?

Oh is there not deep and most wonderful consolation for us in all this? Is it not a riddle to us that we can never answer, why God should love us? Those nearest and dearest to us get out of patience with us sometimes; our most intimate relations and friends know our faults and infirmities best. It is the great difficulty of married life that there can be no concealment of the weaknesses, the failings, which ordinary acquaintances are ignorant of; nothing but deepest love can stand this. Reasonable people may come to the conclusion that there are faults on both sides, and that mutual forbearance is necessary, that man and wife must give and take, bear and forbear. But there is no parallel to this in our relations with God. He sees our imperfections, but He Himself is perfect. There may be motives, wishes, undeveloped schemes, which we hide carefully even from those who know us best; but to God they are all known; He sees the possibilities of shameful deeds lying in embryo within us which favourable circumstances would bring out into ghastly deeds. A look through a microscope will often make us shudder, but the eye of God sees more perfectly the thoughts and intents of the heart, and yet He is patient with us, He still loves us. We do not half realise this. The great God has so stooped down to our level; He has so often used human language that we get to treat Him as if He were but a man. If we can get ourselves into a certain state of feeling we are quite satisfied to come into His presence without any cleansing of our hearts. The common phrase about not being "fit to come to Holy Communion" is an instance of this; people think that some little irritation of temper, or some distraction through business or work, makes them unfit to come, when it is really the innermost recesses of the heart of hearts that God looks at, and not the passing circumstances of the moment. God knows us better than any one else knows us, better than we know ourselves, and with such as we are this can mean nothing else but that He knows a vast amount of sin, of weakness, of utter unworthiness; and yet He loves us. Nothing can fully explain this, no mere reasoning can fathom this mystery. Like many other questions that meet us in the things of God, we must leave this unanswered, and wait till more light is vouchsafed to us.

But there are one or two thoughts that may help us a little way in the meantime. God loves us doubtless because we are His creatures. Creation is one of the initial mysteries that meets us as soon as we begin to think about God and ourselves. We cannot see why God who is perfect in Himself should create anything outside Himself; but assuming the fact of creation, we can see that He would love His *creatures*. It is not easy to realise what it is to be a creature. We can help ourselves a little by analogy; we cannot create anything, but we can make things, and those things are our own absolutely. The artist makes a picture; it is in every sense his own; he can do what he likes with it, alter it, sell it, give it away, let it lie and spoil, destroy it. But he finds pleasure in his work, and regards it in some way as part of himself. What must it be then to create immortal souls that can act freely and return love to their Maker, that can "do the will of their Father in heaven." Can we not faintly imagine how God may love us because we are His creatures? Look at the mother bending over her babe; there is some likeness there of the relationship of the creature to the Creator. God uses the similitude Himself, and says that deeper, more tender even than this, is His regard for us whom He has created. "Can the mother forget her sucking child? Yea, she may forget, yet will not I forget thee."

But there is another reason why God should love us. What costs us most, we value most. The most precious things can only be had in this world by paying a great price for them, and this price is paid with other valuables besides money. Time, labour, suffering, these, when expended upon any person or thing, make it valuable to us. The lost sheep that the shepherd recovers after long and painful search, as our Lord reminds us, is more thought of than the ninety and nine that remained safe in the fold, and gave no such trouble. The poor little sickly child that has scarcely ever left its mother's arms, is the mother's darling after all. The prodigal that returns penniless, shamed, but deeply penitent, is made so much of by the rejoicing father that some are envious and scandalised. If, then, God loves us because we are

His creatures, must not the Son of God love us whom He redeemed with His Precious Blood? Must not the Eternal Father love us for whom He gave His only-Begotten Son? Our lost condition moved the pity of God; and pity is near of kin to love. The destitute and miserable and friendless move our human hearts; the oppressed, the persecuted, find a friend in us. And what so hopeless as our race's ruin? What so desperate as our condition which none but One could save? His love made Him save us, must He not love us still?

But there is one more reason why God loves us; and this is perhaps yet more touching, more comforting, more hopeful to us, because it is more personal, because it comes home to each one of us, and appeals almost irresistibly to our tenderest feelings. We saw just now that God knows us perfectly, that His eye searches our inmost heart with all its thoughts and motives, and we trembled as we felt that all the hidden badness of our character, all our meanness, all our potentiality for evil, was naked and open before Him. But is there not another way of looking at this intimate knowledge of God? Is there not another and an opposite result that comes from this conviction that God looks us through and through? Does He see nothing but evil? Is there no trace left of the image of God in us? Has the grace of Baptism been altogether effaced? Is there no love of truth and purity, no yearning after something higher, something better? The soul may be blind, but is there not a stretching out of the hands as Jesus passeth by; a cry, "Thou Son of David, have mercy on me?" The soul may be leprous, and men may have separated the foul thing from their company, but when no one is near, is there not a creeping up to the merciful One, and a

CHRIST'S BROTHER, SISTER, AND MOTHER.   99

timid plaintive appeal, "Lord, if Thou wilt, Thou canst make me clean?" Even where the lowest depth has been reached, and the unclean spirit has fairly taken possession, does not something impel the poor frenzied incarnation of degraded misery towards the Saviour, till presently the lately demon-ridden man sits at His feet, clothed and in his right mind? Oh yes, we thank God for this; we know the plague of our poor sinful hearts; we know that we are very bad, very weak, very worthless, we never hope to be worth much, we have been disappointed with ourselves so often, but still we are not quite lost yet; God has not yet given us up, God still loves us, still hopes in us, still sees something good in us; Jesus is still stretching out His hand towards us, and saying, "Behold my brother, and sister, and mother!"

What wonderful things have been done by the love of Christ; what transformations from sin to holiness, from death to life! The family likeness long hidden has gradually come out, and the man or the woman has been seen to be the brother or the sister of Jesus, looking like Him, speaking like Him, doing works like Him. Nay, there are greater things than these; the faithful Christian is a brother of Jesus, but there are some greater than he who are like the Mother of Jesus. She found favour with God; she conceived the eternal Word; she gave Him in visible form to the world, to be its Pattern, its Teacher, its Redeemer. Like her are those who are not merely like Christ in themselves, but who bring Christ to others; missioners to heathen abroad, missioners to heathen in-our own land, missioners in their own homes, who like Mary seem to have ever Christ in their arms, stretching forth His Hands to those who come near Him. And He in His wondrous love deems no one beneath His notice, no one too bad to be cared for.

Oh wondrous, blessed thought for such as we are; we who have not been what we ought to have been; we who have fallen very low; we who have been careless and godless, and have found no peace in it all; we who know we might be better and happier; let us turn our eyes and see our Saviour stretching out His Hands to us now, those wounded Hands that were pierced for us upon the bitter Cross. He has not yet turned His back upon us; He has not given us up. If our friends knew what He knows, they would have nothing to say to us; but He knows all, and yet beckons to us to come and be forgiven, and to make a new and better beginning this very day. This is the will of God; the will of our Father in Heaven; He willeth not the death of a sinner, but rather that he should be converted and live. Let His will be done; so shall His Kingdom come to us; and there shall be joy in heaven to-day over the sinner that repenteth, and is saved.

Third Sunday in Advent.

THE MISSION OF THE BAPTIST PERPETUAL.

SCIENCE tells us that the operations of nature have a tendency to repeat themselves, that events happen in cycles, that after a time things return into themselves and begin again, according to some great law that overshadows all minor laws, and bends them into conformity with itself. And since the same God, who made the heavens and the earth, made man also, we shall not be surprised to find the same tendency to uniformity and to repetition in God's dealings with him. So it is that we may trace a general similarity between God's judgments in all times, in His mercies, and in His dealings with men and with nations. It is on this principle that the Church at this season mingles together the two Advents of Christ. There is in some respects the greatest possible difference between the two events, and yet we may trace certain clear lines of similarity, certain broad principles common to both, so that in some respects we may put ourselves in the position of those to whom Christ first came, and range ourselves, either with those who rejected Him, or with those who believed on Him to the saving of their souls.

Let us then take the personal character and the preaching of the Baptist as a general guide to us how we must prepare to meet and receive the Saviour, both here in the commemorative and expectant services of the Church, and also hereafter at the great day when we shall in very deed see Him who was born at Bethlehem.

For four hundred years the stream of inspiration had ceased to flow; there was no prophet, there were no angel visits, no inspired writers. The last notes of prophecy were mysterious. As the silence of the night came on there was an obscure intimation that by and by the "Sun of Righteousness" should arise, and that before the coming of the great expected One, Elijah the prophet should appear, the same stern ascetic, the same bold reprover of sin, the same terrible herald of judgment as heretofore.

What is our present condition? Singularly similar. Our Scriptures, like the Scriptures then, are sealed up and closed, and as then, so now, the last page tells of the coming of Christ, "Behold, I come quickly;" the book is finished, and we are now waiting for the coming Messiah.

While men waited there came suddenly down the long-dried channel a stream of mercy from the presence of God. For years there had been nothing supernatural in the Temple worship; all had been done regularly, but there was no voice, there seemed to be none that regarded. To sceptic eyes these rites were empty forms, mere superstitious mummeries. To the faithful they were real ordinances of God, real means of grace. And now the messenger of God vindicated their faith.

Again, let us notice what is the position of the Christian Church now. We go on using ordinances and sacraments in pure faith; that one special rite above all we are bidden to observe "till He come." Every celebration of the Holy Communion is like the sacrifices in the Temple, a commemoration of the past and an anticipation of the future. It is a sign that the Church is waiting for her coming Lord.

But when the promise came there was not faith to

receive it; and for a sign Zechariah was struck dumb in the midst of his priestly duties, till his child should be born to be the "voice" of God to His chosen people, and to restore voice to his father. But too true a picture of the Jewish Church before Christ came. It could but "make signs and remain speechless." The rites and ordinances silently proclaimed a message from heaven, for they were ordained by God Himself; they told of a Saviour, of cleansing from sin, of redemption and pardon and the favour of God; but the living voice was wanting. Therefore when John began to preach he declared himself to be this very thing that was needed, a "voice," a voice that could speak intelligibly, that could put into articulate words the mute signs of ordinances long observed, so long that their very meaning had been altogether forgotten or misunderstood.

If we turn to the book of Revelation, and there read of the times of the end, we find that there too it is said there is "silence" before the coming of the Judge; then, too, there follow vocal witnesses preaching to an unwilling world, and like the Baptist sealing their testimony with their blood. In his day Elijah believed himself to be alone; in the days of the end faith shall wax cold; and prophecy tells of apostasy in the Church, and of the triumph of the world and of unbelief; "for that which has been, is that which shall be."

Presently Elizabeth's full time came that she should be delivered, and the infant of promise was born. When the circumcision day was come, they would call him after his father, expecting that he would inherit name and priesthood, and live a quiet ordinary life, as his father had lived. But "old things are passed away." And so for us; to prepare for Christ we must "put off the old man," and have a new name and a new nature. The eighth day of circumcision henceforth tells of the eighth day of resurrection to a new and better life in Christ. Then we are told that "the child grew, and waxed strong in spirit, and was in the wilderness till the day of his showing unto Israel." Here is deep significance, and a lesson never out of date. Holiness of heart and life may be shown unto men, and exercised among them, but it cannot be acquired and formed before men; it requires silence, retirement, and solitude with God. So was Moses trained in the wilderness, so was Israel prepared for Canaan, so was David fitted for his kingdom, and Elijah for his mission. So in the New Testament did St. Paul retire to Arabia before he came forth the apostle of the world, and even Christ Himself retired to the wilderness for a forty days' retreat before He began His work. Is there no need of such retirement now? Are we not too busy to repent; too busy to think of the world to come? Are there not "many coming and going so that we have no leisure"? Is not the advice wholesome for us as for the first disciples, "Let us go into a desert place apart and rest awhile," as during this Advent season.

"The same John had his raiment of camel's hair, and his meat was locusts and wild honey." He lived a hard ascetic life, no soft clothing, no king's palace with its luxuries were his. The way of Christ is the way of peace. His yoke is easy and His burthen is light, but before He is found the way of repentance is sad and bitter.

What do we know of this? We cannot gladly hear of a Saviour from our sins, till we feel our sins heavy and painful; we cannot meet the Judge without fear, unless we have before been reconciled and pardoned. It is because so many have never repented that all is unreal and unstable in their Christian profession.

Let us notice what St. Mark says; his words are most significant: "The beginning of the Gospel of Jesus Christ; as it is written in the prophets; behold, I send my messenger before thy face." Now what does this mean? It means this, that the Gospel of Christ begins not with the sermon at Nazareth, nor with the sermon on the Mount, nor with the Baptism of our Lord, nor even with His Birth; not with Jesus at all, but with St. John Baptist, who makes ready the way for Him. This is a truth often forgotten, often unknown. Men want the harvest without the patient husbandry, the rest without the weary labour. But this may not be. Just so, in order to feel the blessedness of Christ, we must first go and hear John in the wilderness. St. Peter at the first meeting of the Church after our Lord had departed reckons the dispensation as beginning from the baptism of John. There is a yet more important testimony to this truth that John's mission is an essential part of the Christian dispensation. For we read that when our Lord came and began His mission, the people and the publicans believed on Him, but the Pharisees and lawyers rejected Him; and then the reason is given for the difference, that the common people and the publicans had been "baptized with the baptism of John, but that the Pharisees and lawyers had not been baptized by him."

Let us be sure that it is so still. There is indeed this difference in our day, that we were baptized into Christ in infancy, but still we dare not hope to do without John. Many baptized Christians grow up without religion, or relapse into grievous sin, and need absolute conversion as much as those who never heard of Christ. And with the best of us there is ever need of repentance, that is, a going back to the "beginning of the Gospel of Jesus Christ," a searching and examining of our lives and consciences, a going out into the wilderness to hear from the Baptist's mouth wholesome truths about ourselves, not flattering, not even pleasant, but useful, and even necessary, as medicine to purge away evil that lurks within, and to give us an appetite for Christ, the Bread of Life, without which we must die.

Such is the meaning of the Church's institution of the seasons of Advent and Lent before the great festivals of Christmas and Easter; such is the meaning of the Vigils of the holy days. To the careless they seem unmeaning; to the ignorant and prejudiced they seem even superstitious and wrong; but to those who enter into the spirit of the Church, they are gratefully accepted, as the very aids which the frailty of human nature evidently requires, devised by practical men, acting under the influence of Him who knew what was in men. So that the Church's year not only represents in its succession of fasts and festivals the life of Christ her Lord, from the preaching of John to the day of Ascension, but also the life of the Christian, ebbing and flowing like the tide upon the shore, repeatedly going over the same ground, often seeming even to retire and lose what had once been gained, but in the end steadily advancing to the fulness that God has appointed.

Let us then listen to the warnings of John the forerunner; let us submit to his baptism of repentance; let us humbly sit at his feet this Advent, and ask him "What shall we do?"

Monday after the Third Sunday.

THE COMING OF CHRIST'S KINGDOM.

OUR Lord tells us that His true disciples seek first the welfare of His Kingdom, and that human nature, unsanctified, following its own fallen bent, seeks first and last its own welfare. In accordance with this rule He has put into the mouth of His servants a daily prayer, in which, before they ask even for daily bread, and pardon of sin, they pray for the honour of their heavenly Father, and the spread of His dominion. How little is this noticed, how little understood by the many who patter out the words of the Lord's Prayer in public and private so often! "Thy Kingdom come;" what care men about this? "Give us this day our daily bread," even this they deem a needless petition, for do they not look to themselves, their talents, their cunning, their sharp practice, that is so often not quite honest, for success in life? "Forgive us our trespasses," a quite meritorious exclamation on a deathbed after a godless animal life. What then do men ordinarily know or care for this, "Thy Kingdom come?" Mission work is neglected and starved, and men then turn round and say, "What is the good of missions, they do not succeed, we want missions at home." Nothing succeeds without labour, cost, sacrifice, enthusiasm. When men went out with these, missions were no failures. Let us see a great nation throwing its whole weight and heart into missions, and we shall see success. So did Spain conduct missions in the days of her greatness; and with the decay of her mission zeal came decay at home of national vigour and glory. Missions as conducted now will produce results, will bless those especially who in spite of all discouragements promote them, but till men act on the principle of the Lord's Prayer; till they place God's honour first, and write the name of God at the top of every page of life's diary, we have no right to complain of the small success of missions. Countries are conquered, but the Cross is not set up; colonies are annexed, but idolatry is let alone, nay, supported by authority, and scrupulous care is taken lest the degrading superstitions of the people be interfered with. Insult to Christianity is tolerated, humiliating conditions are submitted to, all that trade may flourish. The so-called Christians introduce drink, disease, murderous weapons, tricks of trade; the heathen fight, drink, learn new vices, die off, but they do not become Christian. Would it not be very surprising indeed if they did?

The whole principle of modern thought is antagonistic to the spirit of this prayer. Men have ceased to recognise the sovereignty of God. The world is not God's world; He is not King. The world is our own; we can do what we like with it, and are responsible to none. We must take it as it is, and make the best of it; and when we pass away leave it to those who come after us to do the same. But what is God's account of all this? That the earth is His, with all souls, and all things in it; that man is His Vicegerent to do His will, to rule and subdue in His name, and to render account to Him for all; that Satan and a host of other mighty creatures, having lost heaven, have coveted the earth, and set up in it a usurped dominion, a kingdom antagonistic to God;

that God, who with "one rough word" might vindicate His rights, in His inscrutable wisdom has left His honour in man's hand, and shown him how to recover the world for Him; that after many revelations of this, He sent at last His own Son, not to wrest His rights by force, not to pull down the usurper by divine power from his throne, but to teach man more perfectly God's secret of dominion, the might and majesty of love.

This is what revelation tells us. And what is the testimony of facts and experience? That whenever man has worked in God's way success has followed, that whenever mere human principles have ruled mission-work, such as force and fraud, and half measures that desired dominion and trade and money first, and the spread of God's kingdom only as a means to these ends, there has been failure; that evil is most powerful in the world; that we can almost see the evil ones who rule and ruin God's fair world, almost catch the words of their council chambers, almost map out their schemes and plans. They work upon the innate evil of men's hearts, they offer temporal prosperity as the price of men's souls, they trust chiefly to lies, lies always found out, but always believed again. Among savage people they actually procure their own worship in God's place, and among civilised nations by subtle reasonings work upon highly cultivated minds till they share with them a conscious hatred of, and a deliberate antagonism to, Almighty God. Mighty and clever they are, and yet the little cross-signed Christian child can put them to ignominious flight, and the saints can laugh at them, and hold them up to contempt and scorn, and compel them unwilling to do their bidding. Often the Evil One over-reaches himself, as, for example, in procuring the death of Christ; like the leech that thinks only of gratifying his lust for blood, but the while draws out the poison from the dying man, and saves his life.

Yes, here is our strong hope and resting-place at the sight and under the endurance of evil; men may rage and iniquity may prosper; Satan may reign yet for awhile and desolate the earth; the Church may languish and be evil spoken of, but for all this we stand out and say, "I believe in God the Father Almighty, Maker of heaven and earth;" we kneel down and say, "Our Father, which art in Heaven, hallowed be Thy Name, Thy kingdom come;" we do our duty where He has placed us, and we leave great questions, too deep and high and hard for us, to His infinite wisdom; we trust Him, for He is our Father; we love Him, for we know something of His love for us, and we are sure that He will reign at last, and that all enemies will be put under His feet. The world has wearied itself with masters; Satan has reigned in the person of kings and emperors who have shed oceans of blood and tears, and made the very name of kings hateful; till now mankind is saying it will have them no more, and will rule itself by majorities. Alas! do many fools make a wise man? Do many knaves make an honest man? Is the united voice of many sinful men indeed the voice of the holy eternal Father?

Search the history of mankind, mark the yearnings of humanity, note down the cry of each truth-loving honest soul, then turn to the Gospel of Jesus Christ, and you shall find every want supplied, every desire satisfied. He tells how sin may be pardoned, and the soul purified and restored to peace; He points the way to hope beyond the grave; He shows how evil may be vanquished, and this life made happy. All these have been the much desired boons that the wise and good in all ages have longed for, have sought for. Wherever the records of mankind exist, there are these wants, these desires. And in Christ they are gratified, and in Him alone. His work was enough for all the universe. Wherever there is liberty and reason, there Christ's work extends, its theatre this small world, the spectators and the benefited, the creatures of God in a thousand worlds. Like a poor little insect crawling upon the painted wall of some mighty temple, we little know the purposes, the vast issues, that just touch our small entities in one finite point. "Thy Kingdom come, as it is in heaven," so we pray, as we are bidden; yet we know not what we ask. We work, too, while we pray, but we little know the mighty whole in which it is our great honour to bear a tiny part. God surrounds us and closes us in; His infinite plans go on, and in His wonderful condescension He associates us with Himself in them. The battle with evil rages all over the world, and far away into worlds that we know not. We are like private soldiers lost in the crowd of men, blinded by the smoke, deafened and bewildered by the din of the fight. What know we how the battle goes, how the vast host of God is manœuvred? We cannot see a yard about us; the General does not take us into His counsels; for us it is enough that we are on His side, that we stand firm, or push on, or retreat in good order, in obedience to the word of command. Victory is certain, and He will remember us when He cometh in His Kingdom.

Tuesday after the Third Sunday.

CHRIST'S KINGDOM WITHIN US.

We have already seen the force of the petition, "Thy kingdom come," as it relates to the world at large. But we have by no means exhausted its application and meaning. It is very broad and wide, wide as the world, broad as the stream of time from the beginning till the end. But it is also personal and individual; it can narrow itself down to a point, and focus all its light and heat upon each Christian heart.

"Thy kingdom come;" Where? When? Now, and to thee; for "The kingdom of God is within you." Even the ancients could see that man is a microcosm; in himself a world; small indeed, but complete; small, but not insignificant; small, but the battle-field of the greatest powers; small, but the coveted possessions of mighty rivals; small, but to himself infinitely important and precious. Greece was but a small country, but its people were not only the greatest nation in the world in their own day, but their struggles, their history, their philosophy, their art, their poetry, will interest the world as long as it lasts. Palestine was a small country, but it was the field of God's most intimate relations with mankind. England is a small country, but what is it to us? and what a large share it has monopolised in the history of the modern world.

So with ourselves, great events happen in the world revolutions, discoveries, catastrophes, but after all what touches ourselves individually is really more interesting to us; our little world is our own, and all these external things do not touch us very nearly. This is not selfishness but necessity; it must be so; it ought to be so; it is an instinct of God's implanting. None but a madman wages war against himself; none but a fool is indifferent about the state and security of his soul. If the eternal Father is intensely interested in each soul that He has created; if He valued thy individual soul so vastly that He paid an infinite price to redeem it; if the eternal Son gave Himself for it; what canst thou do and think? What wilt thou give in exchange for thy soul?

All, therefore, that was said of the establishment of God's dominion in the world finds its analogy in thy soul; all the records of the kingdom of Israel, all the parables of the Kingdom of God in the Gospel, have a meaning and fulfilment in the actual or possible experiences of thy soul. The kingdom begins obscurely, but should grow and be perfected, till the Prince of Peace reigns, as Solomon reigned, unrivalled, unconquerable. But, alas! as in God's kingdom of Israel, so in His kingdom within us, there are wars, rebellions, treasons, invasions, usurpers, captivity. Or if we take the analogy of the parables of our Lord, there are debtors to the King, unprofitable and unmerciful servants, rebel lords, guests without the wedding garment; there are tares in the King's fields, foolish virgins in the train of His Bride, lost sheep of His flocks, prodigals and wasteful stewards. All this and much more might be shown at length, for "The kingdom of God is within you." That great spiritual enemy, the guiding power of evil in the world, the Prince of this world by usurpation, he too reigns in the hearts of men where the Kingdom of God should be, and if he be not paramount, he has often his share of the divided heart. There is, as of old, God's Kingdom and Temple at Jerusalem, but schism, idolatry, and rebellion are crowned, successful and secure at Samaria. There are degraded tribes lurking in hills and fastnesses not conquered, driven out and exterminated as might have been, and as God commanded. Do we not know this? and do not these barbarians make raids now and again, and harass us, and beat us sometimes in open field, just as those Philistines terrified and distressed God's kingdom of Israel in old times? Well may we pray then, "Thy kingdom come; Thy kingdom be in me, as it is in Heaven; drive away all enemies, all rebels from my heart, as the rebel host was hurled from heaven; and reign Thou above, my King, and my God! In heaven there is peace, and all hearts bow in willing, glad obedience to the King; all do His will, all worship Him, and hallow His name. Thy kingdom come in me, as it is in heaven."

We were dedicated to God in our Baptism, but is Christ's kingdom really and completely set up in our hearts? Is there undivided allegiance? Is there peace, because the work of conquest is completed, and all enemies are vanquished and slain? In some hearts there is peace, but not this peace. The strong man armed, the successful and undisturbed usurper, the Prince of this world, keepeth his palace, and there is peace; he has made a desert of the garden of the Lord, and calls the silence of ruin peace; if an Elijah forces his way in, he is reproached as a troubler of peace; and if the true and lawful King would get his own again, there is an outcry that he is a pretender, an invading enemy; his ambassadors are insulted, and when he speaks of peace, men make them ready battle. The cry goes forth as at this time, "Behold thy King cometh;"

and at once the rulers are alarmed, and take counsel together against the Lord and against His Anointed. "Let us alone; what have we to do with Thee, O Christ? we have no king but Cæsar. This world is good enough for us; this life suits us, with all its faults; we would be free; we will not have this man to reign over us." Is it not so with men and women not a few? Christ's Kingdom has not come to their hearts; they keep Him out; they admire Him at a distance, but their hearts are their own, and they will have no other Lord there but their own will.

Be our portion with those who pray without reserve, "Thy kingdom come in my heart; as it is in Heaven." The world is very evil; the world has revolted from its Maker and Lord; the Church is distracted and brought low; Christ seems to be once more a homeless wanderer, with no place to lay His Head, a dethroned, friendless, exiled King; but let there be one little realm true to Him, one humble home, like the cottage of Lazarus at Bethany, where the door is always open to Him, where He is ever welcome—thy heart. The King comes meek and lowly; His crown, a Crown of Thorns; there are many wounds upon Him; He seems as if He had been altogether vanquished and shamed in the battle; the world has rejected Him; the great will have nothing to do with Him; the sensual ridicule His rule of self-denial; the clever pick holes in his code of laws. When He is presented to men with the introduction, "Behold your King," the cry is, "Away with Him, crucify Him."

And what say we? Can we stand with the minority on His side? Can we drink of His cup and be baptized with His baptism? If we declare for Him, He will not flatter us.

"If I find Him, if I follow,
What His guerdon here?
Many a sorrow, many a labour,
Many a tear."

His Kingdom is not of this world; its good things are not promised to His servants; nay, He exacts labour as proof of true allegiance; every valley must be raised, every mountain laid low, the crooked must be made straight, and the rough places smooth, for the King's highway, by those who invite Him and say, "Thy Kingdom come." Are we prepared for this? Are we ready to bring every thought to the obedience of Christ? If not, we cannot be His disciples; His Kingdom cannot be set up within us, as it is in heaven. It is not he that saith, "Lord, Lord," but he that doeth all this that gets his prayer granted.

Once more the choice of lords is offered to us; once more the opportunity is given of a new beginning: "Repent, for the kingdom of heaven is at hand." Repent, and return to thy allegiance, if thou hast played the rebel; repent, turn out the usurper, and open the gates of thy heart to thy true liege Lord. Open the gates, and the King will come in and dwell with thee till He takes thee to dwell with Him. Open the gates, strew palms in the way, sing, "Blessed is my King that cometh;" lead the way to God's Temple, and let Him cleanse it from all that defileth, and make it once more the house of prayer, the dwelling-place of God, temple and palace; so only can its sure destruction be prevented in the day of judgment that is coming. Reign He must; all enemies must be put under His feet; He is, and must be "King of Kings;" all must fall before Him, bowing in loving allegiance, or crushed in irresistible anger.

What will we? Shall we be uneasy rebels for a little while, cursed with miserable liberty, ending in swift and tremendous retribution; or wearing His light and easy yoke now, find rest presently and for ever; sharing His Cross and thorny Crown now, enter into the joy of our Lord, when His Kingdom comes with power?

Wednesday after the Third Sunday.

WHAT IS OUR OWN?

THE series of parables of the Prodigal Son, of the Unjust Steward, and of the Rich Man and Lazarus, give us divine instruction on that subject which must be ever present in the mind of every earnest man, respecting which he can scarcely feel he can hear too much, the right use of this present life; how he must live so as to please God, what he must avoid, what are the dangers and temptations that will beset him, and what is the one high principle that must guide him as a clue through the mazes of life, as a compass over the pathless sea of his own experience, now dark with uncertainty, now tossed into threatening waves by the storms of adversity.

In the parable of the Prodigal Son we are warned against intoxicating ourselves with a greedy intemperate use of the good things of this life, and shown the certain miserable reaction of such madness; and yet at the same time there is a blessed hope held out to those who have so wasted time and happiness, and who have the desire and opportunity of repentance afforded them, that there is pardon for them, if they will at once arise and return to their Father. In the parable of the Unjust Steward there is a vivid picture of the way of the world; and from this unlikely subject two spiritual lessons are drawn. There is a steward dishonest, selfish, unscrupulous; there are his lord's debtors, men of the same stamp, for they all fall in with his fraud without the slightest hesitation;

they are benefited by the transaction, they are secured against all risk; that is all they want; they do not trouble themselves about the morality of the act; its evident dishonesty never makes them say a single word of objection; they accept the unrighteous bargain at once. And then there is the lord himself not one whit better than his steward or his clients. For when the steward's trick is discovered he commends its shrewdness; he appreciates the sharp practice, he sympathises with the selfish, unprincipled scheme; probably he owes some of his own wealth to similar transactions; he looks after his own interests, of course; he gets rich, honestly if possible, but still at any rate he will get rich. He sees in the steward a man after his own heart, and admires the knave as one who, like himself, can secure his own advantage in a moment of difficulty, when some one must suffer.

This seems to be the force of this difficult parable, which has been so variously interpreted. There are two lessons deducible from it; one, that we are stewards, and shall have to account to our Master for all we have and are and do; and the other, that we must turn disadvantages to our own advantage; that we must make friends even of the mammon of unrighteousness; that we may be taught even by bad men; that the evil and abominable selfishness of men of the world has its lesson for earnest Christians; that things that seem to be stumbling-blocks in the moral government of the world have yet an inner and spiritual significance; and that the wise can wring instruction, comfort, truth out of them, as the chemist produces precious things from seemingly vile and worthless material.

The third parable, that of the Rich Man and Lazarus,

teaches a lesson on the same subject, the miserable end of selfishness and worldliness, when this short life is over. The Prodigal spends his own recklessly till it is gone, and he is left poor and miserable; the Rich Man is prudent, and enjoys his own till he dies, but then there comes retribution. The Steward uses not his own but his master's property for himself, but he is found out and disgraced; his master is shrewd, unscrupulous, successful, but presently finds his own weapons turned against him, and is served as he has served others.

Such seems to be the connection between the parables, such their common aim and instruction. They point out dangers and fallacies to which every one of us is liable. They tell us of the misuse of God's good gifts to us in this life, and warn us that all such abuse ends in sorrow, shame, and disappointment.

But in the few verses that follow the parable of the Steward there seems to be another and yet deeper truth taught, connected indeed with the subject of the right use of the things of this life, but looking at it from another point of view, and that one less commonly known.

The idea seems to be this. God is the Ruler of the world, not the King of glory only, not simply the Ruler of heaven, but the Master and Lord of this world also; everything is to be referred to Him, not a man's inner life only, but his outward conversation also; not only his religion, but his daily work in his calling; not his Sundays, his prayers, his religious duties only, but his week-days, his business, his dealings with his fellow-men. "We cannot serve two masters;" and in fact none of us has two masters, but one; not two consciences, not two rules of right and wrong, but one. We are either godly or worldly; "he that is faithful in that which is least is faithful also in much, and he that is unjust in the least is unjust also in much." The dishonest man, the dishonourable man, the unscrupulous man, the man who is not upright, diligent, just in his dealings with his fellow-men, is not, and cannot be, a true Christian, whatever his professions may be. These things may be little; nay, they are called emphatically very little, "the least," by comparison with the great and eternal realities of the soul; but if a man is unfaithful in the one, he is unfaithful also in the other. Our characters are made up of many qualities which hang together like the links of a chain, the strength of which is only the strength of the weakest link; or like an arch, any one stone of which being removed, the whole falls to the ground. God is Master in both departments of life. God is trying us now by little things, little responsibilities, little trusts, passing interests; if we fail in these, we shall never be entrusted with greater charges; if we fail in easy tasks, what need to try us with great ones? If we break down under the duties of subordinate positions, how can we expect to be raised higher, and placed in honour and power in the coming Kingdom of God, of which this life is but an imperfect and weak representation?

"If therefore ye have not been faithful in the unrighteous mammon, who will commit to your trust the true riches? And if ye have not been faithful in that which is another man's, who shall give you that which is your own?" Let us notice the force of these words, as connected with the whole subject of the three adjacent parables. See what money, and everything that money will buy, is called; all the good things of life that we have, or may have, all that is attractive in the world to sense or desire. See the remarkable adjective that is used to designate it. In our translation the word is rendered, "that which is another man's," but this does not give the full force of the original word. It means that which belongs to some one else, to any one else, to every one else, that which is common property; just as the air we breathe is common to all; we use it, then another, and so on. So with the things of this life; none of them is ours, except for a moment. Especially this is the case with money, as representing all other good things. The very coin we use teaches us this. It is ours; but it is of no use if we hoard it; it must change hands; its value is only realised when we part with it. It goes hither and thither; it is common to all. Such is money:

"'Twas mine, 'tis his, and has been slave to thousands."

So then this life and all that is in it is not our own, but common to others. Our money, our food, the houses we inhabit, the roads we walk upon, the air we breathe, the light by which we see, the things we handle and use, give and receive, all these things are part of the common stock of the world. We are as guests in an inn tarrying for a day, using the things of others, then passing away and leaving all behind for others to use after us, as others have used them before us. We may even bring this still closer to ourselves, for we cannot call even our bodies our own. Doubtless there is some secret germ that gives identity to each man's body, and will be that which shall be quickened into new life at the Resurrection; but this flesh and blood, these bones and sinews, these limbs and organs, we know what they are; chemists can weigh and measure and assort their ingredients, they can tell us how they are formed of the earth, out of the common material of the world; so that even our bodies are not our own, but their particles may have belonged once to others, and may again belong to others in years to come.

What then is our own? What is it that truly belongs to us, and can never belong to any other, nor be common property? There is first and above all the soul; then there is our inheritance in heaven; and there are riches, stores laid up there, or which may be and ought to be laid up there, things which cannot waste or perish or change, which cannot pass into other hands than our own.

We see now the force of our Lord's words. Here we are in the world, in the midst of things changing and passing away; all things slip through our hands, clasp we them never so tightly; "We brought nothing into the world; we can carry nothing out." We are stewards; we receive from others, and pass on to others all that belongs to this life.

Nor is this all. All the while we live here we are watched; we are on our trial; this is not our home; this is not our life, our vocation. What we shall be, our eternal lot, depends upon what we show ourselves fit for in this term of trial. If we are not faithful in that which is common property, who shall give us that which is our own? Who? There is but One. He who made us; He to whom all things belong, He only can give us our own; and His giving it to us depends on our use of that which is not our own, but which is now entrusted to us. Time wasted will lose us eternity; bodies defiled will destroy the soul; money hoarded, wasted, withheld from right objects, will corrupt and canker the riches that should be our own for ever; this life lost, we lose all.

Our Lord Himself says we may "lose our own soul;" and there is nothing so truly our own as that. If that may be lost, all else that belongs to us may be lost also; and in the great day there shall be no one to give us that which is our own.

Oh the utter desolation of that terrible day for the soul when it finds that it has no part nor inheritance in the world around it! What must the wrecked sailor feel who finds himself upon some barren rock, without shelter or food or companion; he has his life indeed, the waves have spared him that, but of what use is it to him? There is nothing for him but to lie down and die. But what will be the loneliness of the soul, cast up upon the shore of eternity, without a friend, without one thing to call his own, naked, outcast, miserable? There is nothing for him too but to lie down and die, die the second death, from which there is no resurrection.

Let us go forth to our daily duties with these thoughts vivid in our minds:—

> "Thy precious things, whate'er they be,
> That haunt and vex thee, heart and brain,
> Look to the Cross, and thou shalt see
> How thou may'st turn them all to gain."

These bodies of ours that change ever, and shall soon perish, contain within them the germs of immortality; so these little trifles of daily use, of daily duty, contain the seeds of eternal realities. We must not be absorbed in them; we must not despise them; they are not our own, but their right use can give us through Christ that which is our own, that which can make us free and rich and happy for all eternity, lords, princes, potentates, in the one real Kingdom, dowered with unfading honours, girt about with loved and loving ones, who never fail, never turn cold, never die ; having pleasures which may be enjoyed without fear of sin or remorse ; having wealth without danger of misuse, honour without pride in ourselves, and without envy in others.

Thursday after the Third Sunday.

THE DEAD RULE THE WORLD.

WHO or what rules the world? Have we ever thought out this question? Have we made up our minds what is the true answer to it? There is a ready answer that many will give at once: "Kings and queens and governments," they say, "these of course and obviously and without question rule the world; in some cases an absolute monarch, in more a constitutional government, with its prime minister and his colleagues, in them all power is concentrated; they make and unmake laws, they regulate property, they declare war, and presently agree upon terms of peace, they rearrange boundaries of countries, there is no power above them, from them there is no appeal; who cannot see how the world is governed? There is no mystery about it to-day."

But as Solomon says, "He that is first in his own cause seemeth just, but his neighbour cometh and searcheth him;" so it will be replied to what has been alleged: "But who makes the government? Who appoints the prime minister and his colleagues? Who is the master's master? Is it not the people themselves? Their votes determine who shall represent them, their chosen representatives appoint their leaders; the stronger political party has everything in its own hands. It is the people's will that ultimately rules; the majority may be wrong, but they have the right to rule, and no one can stop them; education, property, the best and purest and noblest of mankind are but units, the multitude are generally ignorant, they have little or no stake in the country, they are subject to degrading vices, they are easily led away by plausible and interested demagogues, they are the easy prey of passion, panic, prejudice, but modern wisdom has decided that majorities are always right notwithstanding. Yes, it is the voice of the people that rules the world."

"But," replies another, "we have not yet got to the root of the matter. How are the opinions of the people formed? Who guides, creates public opinion? Is it not the newspaper? Does not the Press rule the world? The Press is anonymous, irresponsible, mercenary, "seated upon a throne of its own manufacture, it summons everything human and divine before its judgment seat; it issues its dogmatic decrees and canonises its own infallibility." Before the invention of printing the pulpit was powerful, but now the newspaper has supplanted the pulpit; what the Pope tried to be and to do, and failed, that the Press has attained for itself; it rules the world, it dictates to kings and governments, it tells us what to believe and what to reject, it defies opposition, and owns no authority higher than itself."

"Not so fast," says another, "there is something yet more powerful than all these, and that is Money. Go to the bottom of things, and you will find in the end that Money rules the world. Money can start and maintain newspapers, or purchase them; Money makes nations powerful; Money is rightly called the 'sinews of war,' and victory now-a-days is generally on the side of the largest and fullest purse. Every man has his price; you can see and feel by your own experience and observation what money can do among those whom you meet, and in matters that you can understand and trace from beginning to end, how can you doubt then that the same influence goes on all the world over; can you question for an instant how the world is ruled? It is ruled by Money."

"You are wrong," replies a grave and respected authority, "money is indeed powerful in this world, but it is not paramount; human nature is not altogether venal, it has always been true, and it is becoming more and more evident every day as education spreads, that 'Knowledge is power.' It is Mind that rules the world. The ignorant are not always rushing blindly where passion drives them; they feel their deficiencies, and come to the wise and crown them king, and make them rule. And what is true of the nation is true of the world; culture tells in the long run; the wise bide their time, and their time always comes; ignorance goes to the wall, and civilisation, which is merely knowledge carried into effect and made general, infallibly gains the day at last, stands in the front, and triumphs over everything else."

Such then are some of the answers to the great question, "Who or what rules the world?" We have seen how each answer combats the allegations of each other, and it is evident that much more might still be said.

But there is another answer to this question, an answer that will surprise the unthinking and those whose judgment is uncultivated, who have not been well taught by knowledge of the world's history, by experience of men and life and thought as they are; an answer that will positively startle many by its paradoxical boldness, and seem to others ridiculous and contrary to reason. It is this: *The Dead rule the World!* "Dead and gone," we say, but in how many cases are we quite wrong when we say so. Is it not true always of the dead that "their works do follow them"? Do we not rightly give the title "immortal" to the great and noble dead, great masters, great inventors, champions of liberty, deep thinkers, heroes in times of crisis and extremity, men whose lives were truly cardinal points in the history of mankind, for upon them events turned as a door turns upon its hinges? The inventors of printing and the steam-engine, did ever world-ruling monarch exercise such wide, such lasting, such still-increasing sway as they? It is well said in proverb that it is the first step that is the important one; when once the new idea is born, it grows naturally, inevitably; but how many ages pass before the particular mind is formed that can give birth to the new idea? A truth once given to the world is a precious investment that ever goes on accumulating and becoming more and more valuable. We boast of our progress, of our superiority to the past, but let us not forget that the most beautiful and elaborate building rests upon buried foundations. All we have and are, we owe to those who have gone before us; they laboured, we enter into their labour; they sowed, we reap; we think we have created new things, but in truth they have but been developed and evolved by natural laws from what came down to us from our predecessors. Look where we may, at science, manufacture, the fine arts, the realm of thought, literature, poetry, the drama, music, politics, we cannot sever ourselves from the men who have gone before us; they are our masters; we are what we are, we have what we call our own, through them.

Yes, it is the Dead who rule the world. Is not each one of us what he is by heredity? Is not the man made from within, rather than from without? Are we not astonished sometimes to find ourselves repeating our father's or our mother's words and opinions, as if they were our own? Do we not catch ourselves in habits of mind and of body that we know come down to us from our parents? Sometimes a leap is made, a generation or two is passed over, and then the family feature, the ancestral characteristic, shows itself again, when it had seemingly been lost. If our fathers thus live and rule in us individuals, is it not an obvious step to take, when we say, that past generations are the real cause of present events, or in other words that the Dead rule the world?

The history of the world is to a large extent the history of a few individuals, representative men who have been new starting points in the annals of mankind. Popular phraseology in the present day makes much of the opinion of the multitude, little of that of individuals; and yet it is not the multitude, but individuals of genius, who have always and who always will rule the world, and make it according to the fashion of their minds and will.

Whose mind and will rule the world to-day? The mind and the will of a dead Man, One who died more than eighteen hundred years ago; the mind and the will of Jesus Christ. Read history, study ancient monuments, recreate in imagination the world as it was before Christ came, and it will be seen how true it is that Jesus Christ is King of Kings and Lord of Lords, that He has been the prophecied Stone that has overthrown the image which represented the kingdoms of the world, and become a great mountain filling the whole earth; that His dominion is from the rising to the setting sun; that the kingdoms of this world have become the kingdom of Christ. He was dead, but He is alive again, and behold "He liveth for evermore." Just as the old inhabitants of Canaan were swept away that the sons of Abraham might possess the promised land, so the ancient civilisation, the world of ages, was swept away by the invasions of the barbarians of the north and east, that the civilization of Christ might be established. Laws, customs, language, the measure of time, modes of thought, besides worship, and the modification of every idea of this life by the new revelation of the life to come, all these date from Anno Domini. The world began again with the new Adam; "He hath made all things new;" He who died on the Cross rules the world.

Perhaps it will not always be so. There are mysterious prophecies of the times of the end, of rebellion against this authority, of the culmination of new principles in the dominion of a new leader of mankind, called Antichrist, who shall "change times and laws," and all else that Christ has laid upon the world. Even now the possibility of this seems growing before our eyes by the rapid upsetting of all things old, by changes that not only startle us by their utter novelty, but by the exceeding rapidity with which they gain favour, and spread and become paramount. We are told by those who are ignorant of prophecy, and even deny its existence and possibility, that the reign of Christ is drawing to an end; we are assured by those whom the world honours as great and learned, and who, it says, speak pure and ungarbled truth only, that the days of liberty are dawning, when man shall be free from the dominion of the benighted past, and shall live emancipated and self-reliant in his glorious present, ever going forward to some still more magnificent future, not in the shadowy world beyond the gate of death, but here, and here only, in this much bettered world, that is good enough for man, and which is the only one he will ever possess.

We have been considering the world at large; as reasonable thinking men we cannot but be interested in it and its destiny, but after all the little world within is yet more interesting, more important to us. We have already seen how much the dead rule there; the great question still remains for each of us whether the dominion of Christ is paramount. He was dead; He died for me; He liveth; do I live the risen life in Him? He is alive for evermore; can I by my own experience say Amen to that?

As the Israelite went up to Jerusalem to worship, he passed on his way many a ruined heap that was once an idol temple, many a lonely crag that was once crowned by some robber's haunt, before God was truly known and rightly adored; before His anointed king made peace in the borders, and drave away lawlessness and outrage from the land. Is this a picture of our hearts? Does the King of Righteousness, the Prince of Peace, reign there, all rebellion subdued, all false gods utterly abolished? They tell us that the animal desires and passions that we feel within us come to us by heredity from our animal progenitors; be this as it may, there is much of the wild beast and the venomous serpent in human nature; has the new Adam tamed them in us, and made the lion to eat straw like the ox? Or better still; in civilized lands the wild beasts are eradicated; is it so in that land within? Does the vine bear fruit well, because there is no wild boar any longer to root it up? The world is perhaps preparing itself to say, "We will not have this Man to reign over us;" in the little world within each one of us, how is it? Is Jesus Christ King there; He that was dead, alive for evermore, ruling unquestioned, ruling by love, giving peace which the world cannot give?

Friday after the Third Sunday.

THE LOVE OF GOD REGENERATE MAN'S INSTINCT.

"THE love of God" is Christ's own description of His religion. To love God above all things is the very motto of the Christian life. Love is the most powerful motive. Love is the pleasantest of all master-powers. It is both easy and pleasant to do what we love. It is no hardship to serve those whom we love. Duty, self-interest, and fear are very powerful influences, but love surpasses them all in the completeness of its conquest, and in the thoroughness of the service it secures. It requires no taskmaster to keep its slaves up to their work; it needs no tempting rewards to stimulate exertion. The servant of love is free, and yet chooses to do his best; he reaps his reward as he goes on, and has no sordid views of future aggrandisement.

True Christianity is the deliberate preference of God to the other masters who bid for our service and affection. The true Christian does what he likes best when he does what God commands; his will accords with God's will. Just as any man looking at the tender loveliness of the tinted sky at sunset, or the violet outlines of distant mountains, or the exquisite pencilling of some hedgerow flower or sea-shore shell, exclaims involuntarily, "Oh how beautiful!" so the purified, enlightened, sanctified soul of the Christian, as he sees God, says also, "Oh how beautiful!" The one is as much an instinct as the other.

No one taught that man by long education to admire the beauty of created things, and that other finds in God's nature the same irresistible attraction. As man's senses were created by God to enjoy the works of God, and to feel pleasure as eye, ear, touch, taste, and smell bring them into contact with himself, so man's moral and spiritual instincts were created to perceive and delight in the attributes of God and His glorious nature. Man was made for this; each one of us was made for this; and in spite of infirmities innumerable, in spite of wayward tastes and selfish follies, we do feel this instinct for God yearning within us for gratification. The very unsatisfaction that makes us hungry and displeased after sinful indulgence; the weariness that we feel sometimes in the midst of much of this world's good things, these are but proofs that nothing less than God Himself is what we really want. We were made for God, and if we give ourselves to anything else we are dissatisfied and unhappy. As the body suffers, if it is placed in a condition that is unnatural, so does the soul of man, if it is shut out from God.

Men love God without knowing it. All that is good and true and beautiful is but part of God. No one is so bad but he admires goodness when he sees it; and all the goodness that we see is but a partial reflection of the nature of God. The unhappiness of our fallen state is this, that those instincts and functions of our nature, which should be subordinate to the one great masterpassion the love of God, have been fostered into abnormal and outrageous development, and keep it down, and almost extinguish it; just as in a neglected garden the choice flowers are overgrown and smothered by the luxuriant and rude rankness of the intrusive weeds.

The curse of sin has desolated God's paradise; the ground indeed brings forth abundantly, but thorns and thistles have now their right of growth, and they very soon get more than their right. It was this ruin that the Son of God came to restore; and so it was significant that when His work was done He first showed Himself in a garden to a penitent, and was by her mistaken for the gardener. He had restored paradise in her heart already; the foul weeds and poisonous undergrowth of sin had been eradicated by His loving power, and God could walk there once more with His creature; for the proper instinct of the soul ruled again, and the love of God was all-powerful and easily first. The seven devils were cast out, and she was restored to her right mind; she loved God, and so was free and happy.

People talk of the precepts of Christianity as unnatural, or even contrary to nature; whereas in truth Christianity does but restore a man to his right mind. We say a man is mad when some idea or ideas that ought to be subordinate become dominant; and since the idea that God intended to be the ruling one in man's soul is the love of God, if that be overmastered, then the man is not in his right mind, and needs spiritual medicine, care, and healing. Christ calls Himself the Physician, come to heal sick mankind. The Creator is the only one who can recreate the wonderful nature of man. He began at the beginning. St. Paul tells us what is the fundamental step in man's regeneration, Christ's sacrament of Baptism. It goes to the root of the matter; man's nature is so corrupt, even at birth, that he must die, and rise again another creature, before there is any hope of his really fulfilling his original vocation. That is the meaning and effect of Baptism; human nature dies, is buried, and rises again in Christ. Christ took our nature that this might be possible. Like Elijah stretching himself upon the child's dead body, His human flesh is joined to ours, face to face, hands to hands; only closer than Elijah could join himself, for we are made one with Him, bone of His bone, flesh of His flesh. Man lost his title to sonship, but now he is adopted again. God is his Father once more, and his one work of life is to love his Father, to return love for love, and to let love teach him what to do, what to leave undone, what to desire, what to live for.

What love of God is, David's passion for his son Absalom shadows forth; ungrateful, rebel, traitor though he was. "O Absalom, my son, my son, would God I had died for thee!" That did God for love of us His rebellious sons. Calvary is the open book of God's love. We must foster and cultivate this love of God. Even when it is implanted in our renewed nature, and the ill weeds are mown down, it is still an exotic that has need of care and culture. We all know that love will grow; we know too that it may wax cold. The lovers of God, like all lovers, frequent His presence, and so feed the flame of love. They are jealous of rivals. All the self-denials and mortifications of the ascetic saints find their explanation in this; they regarded anything that separated them from Him whom they loved, as an enemy to be conquered at all cost. If we think that this is not for us, then let us look at what the saints do and say in another way. Look at Peter, mindful of his infirmity and cowardice, ever repenting of his fall, making no more rash vows of constancy and martyrdom, doubtful of himself evermore, sure only upon one point, "Lord, Thou knowest all things, Thou knowest that I love Thee." Let us adopt His words. Weak we are, and worse than weak; past sins make us not only ashamed, but distrustful of ourselves. What may we not do and be, who have already done what we have done, been what we have been? But still, thank God, deep down in our hearts there is some love of God; yes, real as far as it goes; and there is nothing so sweet to us, nothing so precious; it only wants increase. Let us kneel then with Peter, and say, "Lord, Thou knowest all things, Thou knowest that I love Thee;" and then, "Lord, pour more love into my heart; more and still more, till I love Thee above all things; so only will my heart find rest, so only shall I obtain what I crave for by the insatiable instinct of my nature; so only shall I be satisfied, having all I desire, Thyself."

Saturday after the Third Sunday.

THE HEROISM OF THE SERVICE OF GOD.

EVERY one knows something of that sense of support, that exhilarating confidence, that comes to us when we are items in a great unanimous multitude. It may not be easy to give a good reason for it, but we cannot help feeling stronger and more cheerful when a great many persons are at one with us. The soldier on the hot dusty weary march, and in the heat and horror of battle, is sustained physically and morally by the presence of the serried ranks of his own regiment. A great crowded unanimous public meeting affects both speakers and audience, and creates, by its very atmosphere, a feeling of enthusiasm which cannot be stimulated by most powerful eloquence and the sense of a good cause in a thinly attended gathering. We are unconsciously strengthened in our opinions, or persuaded to change them, by the mere force of numbers. The example, the opinion of the majority is a highly subtle force that always acts upon us, always carries us away with it more or less, just as the currents of the ocean bias and draw aside the ship notwithstanding sails and steam.

On the other hand, who does not know something of the depressing effects of singularity, minority, opposition! The coward yields at once; the brave man feels his cheek chill; the conscientious man begins to doubt whether after all he can be right and all those who oppose him wrong; the man of dogged persistence stands firm to his purpose and position, but the effort saps away all pleasurable feelings, and he holds his own with real suffering. A crowd of thoughts and emotions come into the mind, but they are all painful; there may be energy, self-sacrifice, defiance, but these sentiments are not for the present joyous but rather grievous, destroying peace and tranquillity and all else that are the essential elements of happiness.

There is a very striking and interesting example of this sense of loneliness, of minority, of opposition, in the picturesque account of Elijah in the solitude of the mountain of Horeb. He was a brave man, full of almost reckless courage, quite free from self-indulgent softness. All his life had proved this; but here we see him broken down at last, out of heart. Like a good sword he had hacked and hewed away, as the Arm of God had wielded him against opposing enemies; but now the edge, as it were, is turned, the sharpness blunted, its even keen line jagged and broken. It has had its day; it has been too hardly treated; it is useless for any more fierce brunts of battle. "I, even I only, am left," he cries. Here was the crushing thought; he had lived and worked and witnessed and suffered for God and for truth, but after all, evil was in the ascendant; he had used reason; he had appealed to miracle; he had not scrupled to use force, and to shed blood, and the prophets and priests of Baal had been slain like dogs; but all to no purpose; Jezebel still lived and reigned and was mighty; Baal flourished in spite of all; God and truth were utterly distasteful to the people at large; all were against them and against him; he was left alone, quite alone, and they sought his life to take it away.

Such was the final trial of this great man, and great saint. Nor of him only; every one who has been on God's side in the world has had the same bitter experience in a greater or less degree. Even the most successful leaders and teachers have at some time known what it is to be in a shameful despised minority, and have been humiliated by the sense of seeming utter failure. Their work may have succeeded afterwards, but in their own day there has generally been apparent failure; there have always been times when everything seemed lost, and all their work in vain. Those who read their Bibles know all this; they know by heart the complaints of Moses and of the prophets in the Old Testament, and of the Apostles in the New Testament; and they need not to be reminded of the similar failure of the missions of those of whom less is recorded.

But we need not speak of these; we need not wonder at the perversity of men and the persistency of evil and falsehood, when we remember how the one great Master and Teacher of truth was received, judged, rejected, and at last put out of the way by mankind. Very bitter, very weary, must His human heart have been, as He lived year by year, realising ever more and more the dreadful truth, " I, even I alone, am left, and they seek my life to take it away." Elijah's experience was but a typical foreshadowing of the life of Christ. In Him all the sufferings of the godly culminated; upon Him they were all accumulated. One saint had one part to endure, and another another; but in Jesus all human suffering was consummated at once; " In all our affliction He was afflicted." The Gospels tell us a little; the Psalms tell us more of the cruel agony of that loving heart, as He saw men love darkness rather than light, sin rather than purity, error rather than truth, self rather than God; and confessed His mission a failure.

So then we have come to this; we see one universal law, one uniform experience in all the ministers and advocates of God throughout the history of mankind; this is the unvarying measure that is meted to all; this is God's strange return for hearty sincere self-sacrificing work for Him, sorrow, disappointment, failure! Who does not know something of this? Sunday-school Teachers, District Visitors, men and women who have desired to do something for God and truth and the Church and the bodies and souls of their fellow-sinners, and have done it; and what has been the result? Have they had great success? Have they wrought wonderful results? Have they received the thanks of those whom they worked for; and what they wanted more, their being persuaded to do what they told them; has this been their experience? Surely not. Have they not rather received small thanks for all their efforts, and seen the smallest results from their patient and energetic labours? Have they not been misunderstood and misrepresented? Have they not been disappointed where their hopes seemed best founded? Have they not found themselves in a pitiful minority, in opposition, out of sympathy with others? And have not some of them, because of all this, lost heart, and given up their work? And have not others held back and done nothing, and drifted on day by day with the great tide of easy-going, lifeless, useless people, when there was so much to be done, and when there was such earnest entreaties for help? And what does all this show, but that such persons have not yet read their Bibles to good purpose, have not yet found out God's way with His servants, have not really sought to do His will and to work for Him, but have thought of their own will, of their own honour, their own gratification, or have thought chiefly of present reward and speedy returns, just as if it were some trading adventure that they were engaged in, instead of the high service of the eternal God; and because they have not found these, they have thrown up God's work in disgust, and are now standing idle, and living and spending and being spent for themselves alone?

Those who work for God must learn first of all the spirit of self-sacrifice; they must seek nothing but God's glory; they must expect no reward, but such as their Master received here on earth; they must leave results to God, and be content to be instruments in God's hands, to be done with as He sees best; to have success or failure as He wills; to rise to high place with its anxieties and responsibilities, or to plod on ever in unknown, unhonoured, unthanked drudgery; to be taken up and laid aside without a reason given; in a word, to be as clay in the hands of the potter; to be what the Apostles were, and what they glorified in styling themselves, "the slaves of God," without liberty or rights, His wholly, body, soul, and spirit, His only; and happy and thankful and joyful in the full knowledge and experience of this utter dependence and bondage.

Do we want praise of men, and honour and thanks and testimonials for our good deeds? Our Lord says to us, "Verily I say unto you, ye shall have your reward." If we work for this we shall probably get it. But this, let us remember, is not working for God; it is radically different in principle, totally different in result.

But this is not all. It is not only workers for God who experience this want of success, this loneliness, this sense of opposition to the world around them. It clings to the service and obedience of God in every stage and degree of its development. Our Lord prepared His disciples in every age for this experience. He speaks constantly of the opposition of the world, of minority, singularity, loneliness. Every one that will lead a godly life must be prepared for this. There is a sifting process always going on. The true seed is a residuum. Those who attend the Church services regularly are a minority. These are sifted on week days; sifted again at Communion time. If a man wishes to be in earnest, to carry out his religion fully, to get on in grace, to follow Christ really, he must begin to put himself into a minority; he must learn the sensation of loneliness, separation, opposition. Is not the godly young man in a minority in his office or warehouse? Is not the earnest and consistent young Christian woman in a minority among her giddy, empty-headed companions? Is not the young communicant singular but too often in his own family, literally realising our Lord's own words about those "of his own household"? Is not the working man who does not get drunk an exception? Is not the man who gives away a fair proportion of his earnings to charitable purposes singular, unlike those around him, alone?

What, then, is the outcome of all this? Shall we be deterred from the service of God by the sight of its pains, and by deliberately counting out the cost, piece by piece? God forbid. Rather let it have the effect of enlisting more soldiers in the service of Christ; let it rouse true hearts to a sense that they must be doing more than they are doing; that they are chargeable as idle, sleeping, useless servants; that they have not yet really set out on the way to heaven; that they do not yet know what it is to take up the Cross. Let it be a trumpet-note to call out the heroes and heroines of Christ, not by offers of pleasure and ease, not even by promise of reward, but rather by the stern call of duty, by the evident necessity of pain, of endurance. For what else do brave men and women care for? Is there an expedition to the North Pole, and are not its promoters inundated with offers from volunteers? Is there a forlorn hope in a battle, and are there ever wanting English soldiers to step out of their ranks to join it? Nor men only; are not women ready to vow their lives to God's service, and to live for ever by rule, amidst sin and human degradation, and the sacrifice of all the so-called good things of this life? Yes, it is this daring, enduring spirit, this heroic instinct in the noble human soul, that Christ has laid hold of, and made the very back-bone of His religion. Foolish and self-indulgent people, who know nothing of Christianity, talk sometimes as if religion were an unmanly thing, a thing for women and children, for craven, cowardly, effeminate hearts that cannot do and dare, endure and fight, and be free. Was ever falsehood more deeply false? Who does not know who has tried it that a Christian must be a brave, patient, heroic man, a soldier every inch of him, a man who fights with his own evil lusts, with the strong influences of the world, with the subtle temptations of the evil one? Who does not know that those who are not true Christians are self-indulgent, living for themselves, always taking the easier, pleasanter alternative, shirking all that is unpleasant, hard, self-denying? And what greatness is there in such a course? How can a man be a hero who acts in this way? How can any great and good work be done on such principles?

We live in a self-indulgent age, an age when rule and restraint of all kinds are ever becoming more and more irksome, when liberty is more and more claimed, and indulgence is defended as well as practised. In such an age then the stern example of Elijah is most wholesome. His coarse camel's-hair dress, his rugged unpolished speech, his rough-handed treatment of sin, his life of toil, self-sacrifice, and endurance, here is the pattern for those who would rise above the spirit of the day. Are there not souls for whom all this has charms? Are there not some who are ready to take their stand upon the rock with their weather-beaten, work-stained, care-worn Elijah; ready to bear with him this bitter sense of injustice, of loneliness, of unrewarded labour on the side of God and truth and holiness; positively unable to sink down to cowardly subserviency to the world; unable to give themselves up to ease and softness; unable to tail off after the common herd of selfish, aimless, mean-spirited men and women; unable to serve any other master than the most High God and our dear Father Christ, be His wages what they may? Are there not some whose brave hearts and high instincts compel them to take the noblest way of life, cost what it may, regardless of present reward and pleasure?

To all such the Church appeals; to those the standard of the blessed Cross is lifted up; these are the men after Christ's own heart; He speaks not to them of reward; He claims no sordid service; He appeals to the instinct He Himself has put into their hearts, and bids them come out from the world around them, and follow Him, and leave the idle, the slothful, the sensual, the self-indulgent, to wallow in the pleasures of sin for a season. There must be no bargaining with Him. If a word is said of sitting upon His right and left in His kingdom, He quietly answers, "This is not mine to give; can ye drink of My cup, and be baptized with My baptism?"

Yes, those noble souls must take Christ's side, because they can take no other, no lower. They must take it, not knowing, not asking the reward ; and more than that, not trusting themselves even to think of it, lest the very thought should sully their soul. This is the stuff that saints are made of. Such there have ever been, and ever will be. There are souls everywhere who know what it all means. May they have grace to rise to their high calling, and shaking off all hindrances, to rise up and follow Christ, drawn by resistless love to Him, as the magnet is compelled towards the pole !

Fourth Sunday in Advent.

JOY BECAUSE OF CHRIST'S COMING.

In the Epistle chosen by the Church for this, the last Sunday in Advent, these words occur, " Rejoice; the Lord is at hand." So does the Church bid us prepare for Christmas. The old watchword, that has been repeated over and over again ever since the incoming of sin made the need of a Saviour to be felt, is once more proclaimed, " The Lord is at hand." And with it is given the Christian's reception of the message, the countersign, as it were, to the challenge, "Rejoice." This is the meaning of all Church festivals. They are a mutual drawing together of Christ and the soul, and the result is joy, mutual joy; joy not only to the human soul that is blessed by the presence of its Lord, Who never comes empty-handed to these meetings, but joy to that Lord Himself, whose love is gratified, as love always is gratified, by the presence of the loved one.

We should not forget this. This our Lord is no distant, mighty spirit. He is one of us, a very Man. His human heart swells with joy when it throbs with the quickened pulses of love. We cannot doubt that there is joy in heaven at Christmas as well as upon earth. If there was joy among the angels, as we know there was on the first Christmas day, there must be joy still, and joy in the heart of Him from whom the angels derive all their joy. If there is joy, as we know there is, when sinners repent, there must be joy too when saints draw near to their Lord and He to them, when their spirits, whether in the body or out of the body none can tell, hold communion with Him, and heaven and earth are intermingled, human souls in heaven, angels upon earth, and the Man Christ Jesus with both, His very presence here, not His mere memory, "as it is in heaven."

This is strange and unintelligible language to some. Christmas means joy indeed to them, but mere human joy; may we not even say animal joy, the joy of the creature that eats, lies down in the sun, and sleeps; its few present wants supplied; that has no higher desires, no thought of the future? But if it be not so low as this, yet is it not often mere human joy, the joy that begins and ends with self, and the persons and things that just at the moment cluster round self? The supernatural does not enter into consideration. The door is shut, as of old at Bethlehem on the eve of Christmas; there is no room for the poor wayfarers. One comes and knocks, and goes away; or as the Baptist has it in the Gospel to-day, "There stands One among you whom ye know not."

We may understand the cry, "The Lord is at hand," not merely as coming, but as come; not merely about to manifest Himself visibly and irresistibly, but now manifested spiritually to those who love Him; or actually and really thrust away, rejected as so often of old. The Lord, that is the Master, is at hand; He made us, endowed us with gifts, set us here to work, tries us with evil within and without, and day by day watches us. This is the thought against which the self-willed soul most determinately rebels. It passionately desires to be free, to be its own master, to have no restraints; and so it explains away commands; reasons and argues that it ought to be free, and therefore is free. In the great day of revelation it will surely be seen that this is the great master-sin that underlies almost all unbelief and all unholiness, the rebellion of man's will against the master-will of God. Men huddle up the truth under a confusion of sophistries, but the root of the matter lies in two words, "No Master!" Man hates to have a master; he wants liberty, absolute liberty to know and do evil as well as good; the primeval and never antiquated sin, to have no Lord at hand but himself. Men persuade themselves that they succeed in their wish; for really nothing seems easier. There are Lords many, but really God is the most easily rebelled against of all. There are the laws of health, of society, of our country, of nature, of the sciences, and many more; men bow to the restraints of these more or less; or if they break them they soon feel the consequences and have to pay the penalty; but any one may break the laws of the Supreme Lawgiver with impunity. He is disobeyed, yet does not punish; He is mocked, yet replies not. Men flaunt their rebellion before His face, and say, "If there be a God, let Him take care of His own laws and His own honour;" and still there is no voice nor any that answers; and then they say: "See; there is no God; we may do as we like."

But to-day the Church takes up the well-worn messages, "There standeth one among you whom ye know not;" "The Lord is at hand." It is an old warning; a warning hard to receive; a warning that has round it the incrustations of ancient rejections. Lamech heard it, and argued against it; Cain seemed to escape the murderer's threatened doom, why not he too? Noah preached it before the flood, and "the mighty men that were of old," in the magnificence of their wickedness, proudly and defiantly sinned on. He preached it again, a hoary patriarch, while Nimrod ruled and Babel was being built, and those myriads would own no other "Lord at hand" but him, who was evidently strong, and whose wrath made punishment follow disobedience speedily. Lot preached it on that last morning of Sodom's shameful history, but his sons-in-law turned upon their beds, wearied with last night's debauch, with aching heads and heavy eyes and dull ears, and slept on till the fire devoured them. Daniel preached it at Babylon, while the glowing letters still quivered upon the palace wall in lambent flames; they set him upon a royal horse, they led him in the midnight through the revelling city, they tried to stop his mouth with frenzied adulations, they were so drunk with security and pride and festivity that they did not notice that the great river was failing and its bed running dry, and that with its mighty walls all standing and its hundred gates all shut, Babylon was taken, and the Lord was indeed at hand in judgment.

Who then will believe the Church's Advent message? Jonah-like her messengers may well shrink from the delivery of this ever-despised message, "The Lord is at hand," for the reply is still, "Fool, He is not." The universal chorus of men, the world's verdict, is a flat denial. Old judgments are forgotten, old experiences go for nothing, each generation believes itself wiser than its predecessors. To-day, as heretofore, the message resounds, "The Lord is at hand;" at hand in judgment for the world; at hand in death for each soul; and to-day, as heretofore, the world persuades itself that it will go on for ever, and each man realizes his present life and godlike liberty, and does not realize the thought of death, nor the thought of a present and a coming Lord and Master.

Those only realize it who can give the countersign to the watchman's signal; those who can "rejoice" at the prospect of the Lord's coming; these take just views of life, of death, of judgment. To such He has come already, come often, come in many ways; to them He is no stranger, they know Him well, and what they know does but make them long above all things to know Him better.

"The Lord is at hand," to all, ready and unready, hoping and fearing, rejoicing and hating, at hand to each individual soul. What is this to us? The Judge, the Saviour, He who has been at hand all our life through, and has seen and known all, sins and repentances, temptations, falls, and victories, He is at hand. The end draws on apace; the beginning draws on apace. In Him all things centre; He is beginning and end. Men live without Him, plan and scheme, and leave Him out of their calculations, but to Him they and their lives all come home at last.

Oh that day of strange meetings! that day of surprises! "God was in that place and that, and that, and I knew it not! I thought God was far off, and I have been ever all the while living in the midst of God. I thought death would some day, a long way off, bring me face to face with God; and now I see that my whole life has been Adventide; God has been at hand every day, and all the day long!"

Let us learn this great truth now; now in this our day of learning, and then learn we the next great truth that follows so hard upon it that they two are one, "Rejoice." There is endless lore in those two thoughts; take we them for our life's motto, and they will make us saints, as they have made others before us; "The Lord is at home; Rejoice."

Monday after the Fourth Sunday.

PHARAOH'S BUTLER AND BAKER ADVENT TYPES.

ALL Scripture preaches Christ. In the last verses of St. Luke's Gospel we read that our Lord opened the understanding of His Apostles to see what was written concerning Him "in the law of Moses, in the Prophets, and in the Psalms." In the vision of St. John the Lamb of God opens the sealed book, which was the history of Himself, the revelation of His Name which none knew but Himself, and those whom He Himself taught. For some there are, says the Apostle, who have a veil upon their hearts when they read the Holy Scriptures; they cannot see clearly, they see mere history, mere poetry, while in truth Christ stands in the midst, and they know Him not.

Entering then into this spirit, let us take the story of Joseph and the prisoners in Pharaoh's dungeon, and see how it preaches Christ, how it has an Advent lesson for us, something about both the first and second Advent, joy and sorrow, hope and fear, reward and punishment.

The king of Egypt's servants, it seems, have incurred his displeasure; they are in prison, bound, waiting for punishment, utterly in his power, quite helpless to atone for their sin, or appease his anger. Now here surely there is pictured for us in parable the state of man since the Fall. He has incurred the wrath of God; this world is his prison, and there is a still more fearful prospect of judgment and fiery indignation in the world to come; and nothing can be done, no man can atone for his own sins, nor for those of any one else; each is "tied and bound with the chain of his sin;" he has indeed bread to eat and raiment to put on, but he lives ever in the fear of death, for he has lost the favour of God, the great King.

These prisoners dream each a dream in the dismal night of their imprisonment. They sleep in the cold comfortless dungeon, because they are wearied out; but their sleep is not sweet. They live their life over again in their sleep, and when they wake they are more sad than ever. They are filled with strange thoughts and fears which they cannot interpret; they desire above all things to know their fate, but none can tell them. Just so is man by nature; just like this were the thoughts and forebodings of the Greeks and Romans and other heathen nations, who had lost the knowledge of God, and yet were ever "feeling after Him, if haply they might find Him;" if perhaps they might learn what they were, whence they came, and whither they were going. As we read their writings we feel as if we could almost look into their faces, and see them bewildered and sad; for their life is to them but a dream, a riddle, a puzzle, and there is no interpreter of it for them.

Now there is another person introduced. He is a servant like the others, in prison like them, yet invested with authority, endowed with divine wisdom, able to tell them all that they so much desire to know. He has done no wrong, yet he is disgraced and punished; he suffers for another's fault; he might have escaped and lived in honour, but he would not. "Is not this the Christ?" He took upon Him our flesh, and came in the likeness of men; He humbled Himself to the lowest place, and assumed the form of a servant, for very mercy. He became as the weak, that He might save the weak. He entered the prison, that he might set the prisoners free. Yet not all; for now we must notice that there are two prisoners, with different dreams, and very different fates. So it is all through the Bible. "One is taken, the other left;" Abel and Cain, Jacob and Esau, David and Saul; down to Peter and Judas, and the two thieves crucified with our Lord.

The first dreamer, the king's butler, or more correctly his cupbearer, dreams of his life; he sees a vine, it buds, it blossoms, till clusters of ripe grapes hang thick upon it. Pharaoh's cup is in his hand, he plucks the grapes, he presses the juice into the cup, and humbly presents it to Pharaoh, who accepts it. This dream is a life, and what sort of a life? An active, faithful, watchful, dutiful life. The servant is not doing his own will, but his lord's; he is not idle but careful; he does not sleep, but waits and watches; and when the fit time comes, acts and does his duty, the work set him by his lord. The vine has no grapes at first, but only branches; then leaves, then blossoms, and lastly the gradually maturing fruit; and this fruit is crushed that its sweetness may come forth, and be fit for the king to accept.

The vine is constantly used in the Bible as a type of peoples or individuals, "Thou hast brought a vine out of Egypt, Thou hast cast out the heathen and planted it;" "The vineyard of the Lord of Hosts is the house of Israel;" "I am the Vine, ye are the branches." God, our Father and Master, the Lord of the vineyard, looks for fruit in us; yet that fruit must come gradually, must be waited for patiently; must be sought for with much labour, much care, with digging, dunging, pruning, weeding, watering, watching. The cup of the Great King is in our hand, to tell us what He expects of us, fruit, good fruit, sweet, ripe, mature fruit, fruit at the due season, when He comes to seek it, that He may drink the new wine with His chosen servants in His Kingdom.

Jesus, the better Joseph, came to tell glad tidings to those who thus diligently did the will of God, that their labour was not in vain, that their work should be accepted, that they should soon be brought out of prison, be freed from the bondage of this death, and after three days, that is the time of Christ's resting in the grave, they should have a joyful resurrection, and so their high calling should be restored to them which Adam's sin had lost them; and thus should they be evermore with the Lord. Thus did Christ tell men their dreams. There were among the heathen many God-fearing, virtue-loving, virtue-practising men and women. St. Peter says that Christ went and preached to the spirits in prison, was it not to these? These who had lived according to the law without the law; these who like Cornelius feared God and did His will, though they knew not Christ. To these, waiting for the resurrection, Christ explained their dreams, and promised a speedy and a happy deliverance. The same Gospel is preached to us, to those who are like the chief butler; to those who by patient continuance in well-doing seek for glory and honour and immortality, it tells of and promises eternal life; but to those who do not obey the truth, but obey unrighteousness, even the Gospel of glad tidings tells of indignation and wrath, tribulation and anguish.

This brings us to the second dreamer; he too dreams

of his life; he is Pharaoh's baker, and his duty is to provide baked meats for the king. But what does he do? He prepares baked meats indeed; but he puts them into "Baskets with holes;" for, as the margin tells us, this is the true force and meaning of the words. And he puts these baskets on his head; that is, in a place where he can neither see them nor protect them. The consequence is that the wild birds light upon the baskets, and devour the meats, and he does not notice them; or the meats drop through the holes, for he cannot see them; and so they are lost, and become an easy prey.

Are we not at once reminded of the seed upon the stony ground in our Lord's parable of the Sower? The ground was not fit to receive the seed, it was therefore trodden down of men, and devoured by the birds of the air. There was the same seed, the same sower, the same rain and sunshine, but some seed brings forth good fruit, and some is devoured by birds. The butler and baker both worked, the former acceptably, the latter in vain. And his punishment is noteworthy. The birds that devoured his work that should have satisfied his master, presently devour his flesh as he hangs dead upon a tree. May we not see his fault indicated by his punishment? For, Job says, "They that plough iniquity and sow wickedness, reap the same." A man's sins are their own punishment; what he sows he reaps. If he sows to the flesh, he suffers in the flesh, and reaps corruption. Are we not taught then that this man had lived for himself, had been careful about his own affairs, careless about his master's? His master's work was carried in a "Basket with holes," and so was lost and wasted.

Here then is the worldly, careless Christian; here is the dream of his life, interpreted and set before him by

Him who is "The discerner of the thoughts and intents of the heart;" He who not only will hereafter sit as a refiner, separating the gold from the dross, but who does it even now, for the warning or encouragement of those with whom He has to do. These careless people work and labour and toil; they clutch fast that which they can gather for themselves, be it little or much; but the things of God are put into a "Basket with holes," out of sight, above their heads, and their eyes are toward the earth; and so they lose all; and when they come before the king, they will have nothing to present to Him. They have made provision for the flesh, but are not rich toward God; they have no treasure in heaven; in this life they seem prosperous, and full, and enviable; but they shall carry nothing away with them when they die, and shall stand naked and empty and filthy and shamed before their Lord and Judge.

Have we not here then a striking lesson for us all? We fancy sometimes that we are free, our own masters; that we can live as we like, neglect duties and forget it; do our own will; go our own way, and ask no one's leave; give account of ourselves to no one. But it is not so; we are only servants after all; we have our work and duty; our Master has set us to work, and has gone away, but He will come again. There will be a day of reckoning; reward and honour and joy for the diligent and faithful servant, punishment and shame and bitter regrets for the idle, dishonest, and disobedient servant. The first and second Advents are mingled, as the Church always sees them; the birthday of the King, and the judgment of His true and of His wicked servants. The Birthday of our King is near; the Birthday in humility and poverty, yet He will make a feast to all His servants, a spiritual feast, to which He bids all "that are religiously and devoutly disposed;" all His servants, not a few but all; the feast is provided for all; He expects all. And yet we must not think only of His Birthday, but of the great Second Coming, when, like Pharaoh, He will reward and punish His servants according to their works.

But in the meantime He sends a Joseph to us; He tells us our dreams, shows us ourselves, our life, and our end, in the mirror of the Word of God, as St. James calls it. And not only so, but helping our infirmities, giving us grace and pardon and strength, if we will have them, to prepare us for that great feast that He will hereafter make for all His faithful servants.

His Birthday is at hand; a day kept with joy perhaps by angels in heaven, a day dear to the loving heart of Jesus, a day when He will be ready to give, glad to pardon. Let us prepare to meet Him on that day, that we may be ready to meet Him on His Second Advent day. And how shall we prepare to meet Him? Even as He prepared Himself to come to us, in great humility, as a little Child. He who dwelleth in highest heaven and inhabiteth eternity, He cometh to dwell with us, in us, if we are of a humble and contrite spirit, "to revive the spirit of the humble, and to revive the heart of the contrite ones."

And what shall we bring Him? What birthday gift shall we offer in return for so much from Him? Oh, wondrous exchange! we need but bring Him our sorrows, our miseries, our sins, and cast them down at His feet, as He lies in the manger, and through His grace leave them there. We need but bring Him our emptiness, and He will give us of His fulness; bring Him broken hearts, that He may bind them up; that they may be remade as vessels of His glory to contain Himself, like the chief butler's cup filled with sweet wine, acceptable even to the great king his lord. And He will feed us with His Body, which He took as at this time that It might be broken for us; and He will wash us with His own Blood, which He shed for the remission of sins; and gladden us with the new wine of His Spirit, till this life is past, and we have lain for a little while in the prison of death; then shall He come to us on the resurrection morning, as Joseph came to the prisoners, and tell us the joyful news that the prison shall no longer confine us, that the King has pardoned us, that He expects us at His royal banquet, that He will never more be angry with us, but that we shall dwell with Him for evermore, in peace and love and joy.

Tuesday after the Fourth Sunday.

EVIL.

THE parable of the Tares touches upon that great mystery of mysteries, the existence of Evil in the creation of God. It does not even hint at an explanation of it, but it declares God's will respecting it, that so it is to be till the end. Good and bad flourish side by side in the world; God knows it; God interferes not; He says only, "Let both grow together until the harvest." God is Almighty; God is good; and yet misery reigns widely in God's world; evil prevails; wrong by might masters right; the good suffer, the wicked triumph, and yet God does not interfere. He is not ignorant of all this; much less is He indifferent to it; but He says, "An enemy hath done this; let both grow together till the harvest." Yes, "grow," for as good grows, so grows evil also. Civilisation spreads blessings, but side by side grows the evil also, new evil, unknown till the new good was known, and both grow together. Much is ours which was not enjoyed by our fathers; we magnify our privileges and modern advantages; and sometimes mistake mere comfort or luxuries for real and substantial progress. But we know quite well that the good we enjoy is no more unmixed good than was that of past generations. We know the tottering weakness of this great modern civilisation; the head is gold indeed, but the feet, the foundations of the whole, are clay. We rejoice with trembling, seeing greatness and weakness so mingled together, the elements of discord and decay "growing together" with the principles of liberty, of knowledge and material prosperity.

"The world seems simply to give the lie to the great truth that there is an Almighty and all good God. If I looked into a mirror and did not see my face, I should have the same sort of feeling which actually comes over me when I look into this busy living world, and see no reflection of its Creator. To consider the world in its length and breadth, the greatness and littleness of man, his far-reaching aims, his short duration, the curtain hung over his futurity, the defeat of good, the success of evil, physical pain, mental anguish, the prevalence and intensity of sin, the dreary hopeless irreligion, all this is a vision to dizzy and appal. What can be said, but either there is no Creator, or this living society of men is discarded from His presence? Did I see a boy of good make and mind, with tokens of a refined nature, cast upon the world, without provision, unable to say whence he came, his birthplace or his family connections, I should conclude that there was some mystery connected with his history. And so I argue about the world; if there is a God, since there is a God, the human race is implicated in some terrible aboriginal calamity; it is out of joint with the purposes of its Creator." Thus then we find the first meaning of the parable, "The field is the world;" but an enemy hath sown thorns and briars in that which God blessed and declared good. "All the foundations of the earth are out of course."

But there is another application, and that a yet more strange and unexpected one. "The field is the world," but the Gospel message is to all the world; Christ's

Church is Catholic, co-extensive with the world, so at least in the Founder's intention and charter, so in theory, nothing less. This parable is then a prophetic declaration of the history of the Church. It was a hard sentence; earnest men in primitive times almost rejected it, as loving Peter almost rejected the hard sentence of humiliation which His Lord passed on Himself, "This shall not be to Thee." Was not the Church to be holy, pure, triumphant, the body of Christ, free from sin, unspotted by the world, the very household of God? And when sin was seen in Christians, and error was rampant in the Church; when even priests and Bishops were worldly-minded and un-Christ-like, then good men sighed and were discouraged, for if the Church failed, where should they look for truth and light and purity? Then too wicked men rejoiced, and found apology and countenance for their own sins in the weaknesses and infirmities of those who professed a higher rule of life, and supernatural aids to holiness. Then also restless men made divisions, and separated from the imperfect Catholic Church, that they might form for themselves a perfectly holy sect, with higher attainments and more stringent rules. Students of Church history know how keen was this controversy in the early ages, and they know too how the great Augustine, Bible in hand, allayed the hideous discord, and how this and other like parables were mighty in his use of them, how he proved that such a sad state of error and weakness was but that which the great Author and Head of the Church had foreseen and foretold, and that schism was not justified by it, as indeed it was proved to be no remedy for the evil complained of. He said, "Here, as Christ foretold, are the Tares growing together with the wheat; here are the bad, worthless fish in the net with the good fish; here is the chaff with the wheat; here are foolish virgins with the wise, idle servants with faithful, goats with sheep, fruitless trees with fruitful. So it must be till the end. As the Ark held clean and unclean beasts; as Israel contained a mixed multitude, not of Israel; as the Bible from the beginning tells of good and evil mingled, of everything with which man has to do reflecting man's infirmities, man's double nature, good and bad, so must it be even in the Holy Catholic Church; so till the end of time, so till the Lord come to reckon with His servants, to visit His vineyard, to gather in His harvest, to separate sheep from goats, wheat from husks, corn from tares; to present to His Father a glorious Church, not having spot or wrinkle or any such thing."

That which Augustine taught out of God's Word is no less needful to be taught now. If it were better understood—this inevitable imperfection of the Church on earth—good and earnest men would stay with her and help her, instead of separating from her, and weakening her; yes, and doing the enemy's work all too well, by dividing the strength and the hearts and the labours of Christ's true servants, and so hindering the great work of Christ in the world, which, if Christians were united, would go on and abound as He intended it should do. "It must needs be," says our Lord, "that offences come, but woe to him by whom they come." Woe to those who cause divisions and maintain schisms; woe to those who keep down the advance of the Church in spirituality and holiness by the unholiness and worldliness of their lives within the Church; woe above all to those in high places who should be the protectors, the guides, the reformers of the Church, and who do none of these things.

Let the parable teach us this also, that if active error

is bad, mere slovenliness and sloth are worse, more common, more mischievous. It is "while men sleep" that the enemy comes and sows his tares. They sleep through mere idleness, when they have much work to do; they sleep as the evil steward slept, wearied with unhallowed revelling. And even if it be not so bad as this, yet still this sleeping is the source of evil to Christ's Church; sleeping as Peter and his fellows slept, when they should have been praying, instead of giving way to weariness and sorrow. Has not the sleepless enemy a time of vantage over men, who must of necessity sleep, and who may at right times sleep without sin; and yet while they sleep the evil comes in and grows, because here there can be no perfection?

But in the midst of all this that is so sad and so humbling, let us not pass over one good word of hope. These tares that grow with the wheat, we are told, are a sort of degenerate wheat; culture and care and time can convert them into true wheat, as good as the produce of the good seed. Here then is encouragement in the midst of so much that is disappointing and depressing. The sinner may be converted from the error of his way; the schismatic may be reclaimed; the slothful may be stirred up to activity and usefulness. In the Ark of Christ's Church the wolf that entered may come forth a lamb, the raven may be changed into a dove; or, as another parable tells us, the Gospel leaven may work and spread, till it reaches that which seems hopelessly dead. This gives a new force to the prohibition against rooting up the tares before the harvest time. Zealous men in all ages have need to be reminded of this; even Apostles wished to call down fire from heaven upon those who denied their Lord; and in later times we know how axe and stake and dungeon were thought the best instruments for propagating the truth and eradicating error, instead of that spirit of meekness and forbearance, after the example of our Lord.

But let not the godless and careless mistake this leniency of God and of the godly. At present they are let alone; at present they are none the worse for irreligion; sin prospers, its pleasures are sweet; sinners laugh and enjoy their liberty, and live as they list and lust, and no harm comes to them. The same things seem to happen to all. The worldly are no worse off than the godly, but rather better on the whole. Yes, so says the parable, "Let both grow together;" wheat and tares grow side by side in the same field; the same sun warms and gladdens both; the same showers refresh and invigorate both. As the soft summer breeze steals across the field, tares and wheat alike bend to it and rise again with equal grace. But summer lasts not all the year. The autumn comes, and with it the harvest. The reaper comes; the reaper Death; and after death the Judgment; "Bind them in bundles to burn them." O day of wrath! O day of mourning for tares, for unpardoned sinners; for Dives who has had his good things in this life; for those who would not be saved in spite of Calvary and the mercy of God!

But we must find yet a third interpretation of this parable. We have seen its application to the world at large and to the Church; we must bring it closer home yet. For, says our Lord, this Kingdom of heaven, of which the parable speaks, is within us. The field is the world, and yet man is a world in himself. There is a world within him as well as without him. The preceding parable proves this; for where the seed is cast, where the birds prey, and the thorns grow, and the stony ground is fruitless, is, we are told, all within man's heart. Here too the enemy sows tares; here they must grow their bitter growth till the harvest. Do we need to have this proved to us? Do we not know what contradictions of good and evil there are within us, till we are a mystery and a paradox even to ourselves? Those horrible devilish thoughts that rise up in our minds sometimes, envy, spite, revenge, jealousy, selfishness, self-conceit, those mean and despicable feelings that we hate even while we indulge in them, what can we say but that "An enemy hath done this"? And yet there is good in us, love of truth and goodness and purity, power to be good and to do good; surely this field of mingled crops of wheat and tares is within us; and we are told that both must grow together till the harvest. We may not, cannot root up those noxious weeds; only we may strive by good culture to sweeten them, and develop them into good wheat. But still, on the whole, such as we are we must be content to be. This is our trial, not only to live in the midst of evil, not only to lament imperfection in the Church, but even to the end to grieve over imperfection and sin in ourselves, do what we will by labour, receive what we may by grace. We are bewildered and baffled, and sometimes made very miserable at the sight of the empire of evil and its cruel work in God's world, in Christ's Church, and in our own poor hearts; the best antidote is that which Christ Himself commends, the faith of a child in what his father does, trusting his wisdom and love, when the reason is not given, and cannot be understood.

> "All nature is but art unknown to thee,
> All chance direction which thou canst not see,
> All discord harmony not understood,
> All partial evil universal good;
> And spite of pride in erring reason's spite,
> One truth is clear; whatever is is right."

Yes, this faith is our one stay in the midst of all the evil in the world, in the Church, in ourselves. Evil is not eternal; good is eternal; evil will have its day, and do its work, and then come to an end. Death and Hell shall be cast into the bottomless pit, and God's servants shall be free. The rod of discipline shall be cast away; the time of probation shall end; we shall know as we are known. "Till the harvest" we wait and suffer and work and hope. "Till the harvest;" then the tares shall be rooted up, and no more vex the wheat; then evil shall be done away for ever, and God alone, the One Good, reign supreme, and the godly with Him.

We sometimes wonder how such as we can ever be with God, or be happy in His awful presence in heaven. Let us find hope here; "We shall be changed." How much that we now lament and are ashamed of in ourselves may be due to the sinful flesh that we inhabit. Medical science is daily showing how much the body affects the soul, how strangely some little physical defect or disease or injury acts upon brain and mind, and so turns the man almost into another and opposite being. How much then may not be left in the ground when we rise in the likeness of Christ's resurrection; when at last and for ever by Him, Who "discerneth even to the dividing of soul and spirit and of the joints and marrow," evil shall be searched out and separated from the good, the tares from the wheat, and God's true servants shall at last be that which they have ever wished and striven to be.

St. Thomas.

THE ADVENT LESSONS OF ST. THOMAS'S DAY.

THE position of St. Thomas's Day is peculiar. We should rather have expected that it would have been placed near Easter Day than Christmas Day. Perhaps it was appointed to be observed on this particular day because his martyrdom actually took place on it. If so, since the Christians of the first age called the day of a martyr's death his Birthday, there is an evident fitness, even if it be but a coincidence, for the place of St. Thomas's Birthday near the Birthday of Him whom He adoringly called his Lord and his God. Martyrs cluster round Christmas Day, St. Stephen the Protomartyr, St. John the martyr in will but not in fact, and the Holy Innocents, martyrs in fact but not in will. It is well then that St. Thomas too should be there, "doubting Thomas," that all may see that weak faith and a desponding heart may by God's grace be made strong as the strongest, and that he who has failed need not despair, but may win the crown of glory, and take his place at last with the saints when His Lord cometh in His Kingdom.

But we may discover other good reasons for commemorating St. Thomas at this time. Was not this sudden appearing of Christ in the upper chamber an Advent? Are there not always certain points of resemblance between all the Advents of Christ? We are told that the Great Day will come upon men unexpectedly, "like a thief" in the night. The parable of the Virgins relates that there was a cry at midnight, "Behold the Bridegroom cometh." So the coming of Christ to meet Thomas was sudden, unexpected, and in the night. Then our Lord says, "When the Son of man cometh, shall He find faith on the earth?" Want of faith was St. Thomas's fault. Faith is equally necessary for belief in our Lord's Incarnation and His Resurrection.

Once more, St. Thomas continued in misery and loneliness so long as he kept away from the assembly of the faithful; it was when the disciples of Christ were gathered together in His name, that He came into their midst, and gave His peace to St. Thomas with the rest. Just as Simeon and Anna after long waiting at last found their Lord in the Temple of God; just as our Lord's Mother found Him there after that three days' dreadful loss and dreary search among kinsfolk and acquaintance, so must we wait for our Lord in His Temple, so may we look for the fulfilment of His promise to come among us "when two or three are gathered together in His Name," so must we "not forsake the assembling of ourselves together, especially as we see the Day approaching."

Our Lord's greeting to St. Thomas and the rest was, "Peace be unto you." At His first Advent "Peace" had been proclaimed by the angels. At His Advent to each pardoned soul in death He makes it depart in peace, and rest in peace; and we believe that His last Advent will still be the same, and that the risen saint when he meets His Lord will hear the same gracious greeting, "Peace be unto you." It was peace that St. Thomas sorely needed.

Every recorded saying of his indicates despondency. He was ready to die with Christ, but he could not bear up against wearing anxiety and temptation to despair. He nursed his grief in solitude, but as soon as he joined the company of the faithful he found peace. In these days when our Lord has gone away, and we are waiting and looking for His second Advent, we too are often tempted to despondency. Let us see its danger from the example of St. Thomas, and seek its cure where his was cured.

It was the sight of our Lord's Passion Wounds that restored the faith of St. Thomas; and when Christ shall come again in His glory those Wounds will be seen; all will recognise Him by them; the dread Judge will be " Him that was pierced."

> " Those dear tokens of His Passion
> Still His dazzling Body bears,
> Cause of endless exultation
> To His ransomed worshippers."

In this our time of waiting and watching for His Advent, His Wounds are our plea and hope. St. John in his vision saw his Lord before the Throne, " A Lamb as it had been slain." The Hands which He lifts up to intercede for us are pierced Hands; the Hands with which He blesses us are pierced Hands. And as He is, so must we be. Though we are risen with Him we must " Bear about in us the dying of the Lord Jesus." It is by " the marks of the Lord Jesus," that we are known to be His disciples. We must be " crucified with Him," that we may be with Him in His Kingdom.

There is another point of similarity between the circumstances of the Nativity and our Lord's appearance to St. Thomas. It was a marvellous act of condescension that our Lord should take such pains to convince His one faithless disciple, and it was indeed an act of condescension beyond all understanding that He should come into the world as a little Child. The Good Shepherd not only gives His life for the sheep, but He knows every one of them, and calls each by name, and if but one be lost He goes after it till He finds it. It was "for the more confirmation of the faith" that St. Thomas was suffered to be doubtful for a time; let us "perfectly and without all doubt believe in Jesus Christ," not merely in the fact of His Resurrection, but in His marvellous love to each soul, even the desponding and the weak in faith, as taught by His tender condescension to St. Thomas. Let us contemplate this to-day, and we shall be prepared to see greater things than this on Christmas Day, so that like St. Thomas we shall be able to say no more than "My Lord and my God," and silently worship and adore.

When our Lord met St. Thomas, He repeated to Him his own words. Just as He had astonished and converted Nathanael by telling him that He had seen him under the fig-tree, so He convinced St. Thomas by showing him that He had heard what he had said of Him to the other disciples. This, too, seems to possess an Advent significance. This same Jesus will be our Judge, and He will know and recall to our remembrance our deeds, our omissions, our words, our thoughts. All things are naked and open to Him; in Him we live and move and have our being. To Him let us go for pardon of every sin now, that when He sits as Judge there may be none for His justice to condemn.

Advent is nearly over. Another season of Grace is passing away. Have we been "reconciled to God"? Do we keep away from Him? Are we still strangers to

Him? Advent reminds us of the day when He will say to some, "I never knew you; depart from Me!" All their life long they have said, "Depart from us; what have we to do with Thee?" They have kept away from the company of the faithful, they have "not been with them when Jesus came." The Judgment Day does but ratify their life's choice. The sentence is their own. Their own words are remembered and repeated to them as their sentence. "By thy words shalt thou be justified, or by thy words shalt thou be condemned."

Oh let our place be with St. Thomas; let us throw ourselves at those pierced Feet crying, "My Lord and my God;" with not one word of defence or excuse; we see that He knows all; we lie at His Feet in the attitude of penitence, in silent confession of guilt, in silent craving for pardon. Those few words have expressed all our soul's thoughts, past failure, present conversion, resolve for the rest of life even to the end. "My Lord;" my Master Whom I was pledged to serve, Whom I have disobeyed, forsaken, serving other lords; henceforth my sole Lord and Master; and I His servant, His willing slave, bought with His Blood. "My God," that I may "believe in Him, fear Him, love Him with all my heart, with all my mind, with all my soul, and with all my strength; worship Him, give Him thanks, put my whole trust in Him, call upon Him, honour His holy Name and His Word, and serve Him truly all the days of my life."

Thursday after the Fourth Sunday.

THE REWARD OF WORK FOR GOD.

THE thought of Judgment is for the most part a thought of terror. The strictness of the scrutiny, the unalterable finality of the sentence, the awful nature of the doom of the condemned, these fill the mind with terrible fears, when it sets itself to meditate at Adventide upon the Last Things. But there are other thoughts proper for this season, and the parables of our Lord provide them. There are the wise Virgins, who were ready for their Lord, and entered with Him into the bright and sumptuous bridal-feast. There are the faithful Servants, who used rightly and well the Talents and the Pounds. There is the Steward, whom his Lord finds watching when He comes, who can render a good account of his stewardship, and is blessed. There are the guests clothed in the Wedding Garment, who have no fault found with them, while the intruder is discovered and turned out with ignominy. Our Lord Himself bids His true disciples "Lift up their heads," when the signs of His second coming are apparent, because their redemption draweth nigh. Almost the last words of the New Testament are, "Come, Lord Jesus;" and He has bidden us pray unceasingly, "Thy Kingdom come."

This is an aspect of Advent that we must not forget. We ought to be able to enter into this feeling. The

Church puts into our mouths a prayer on the last Sunday in Advent, asking God to "come among us," and bids us "Rejoice, because the Lord is at hand." The child rejoices at the near prospect of his father's return; the wife counts the hours till her husband comes; and we are the children of God, and the soul is the bride of Christ. Then the second Advent will be the end of sin, of suffering, of doubt. It will be the restitution of all things, the revelation of light and truth; we may well pray for it, long for it:—

> "Oh, quickly come, dread Judge of all;
> For awful though Thine Advent be,
> All shadows from the truth will fall,
> And falsehood die in sight of Thee.
> Oh, quickly come; for doubt and fear
> Like clouds dissolve when Thou art near.
> Oh, quickly come, true Life of all;
> For death is mighty all around.
> On every hand His shadows fall,
> On every heart His mark is found.
> Oh, quickly come, for grief and pain
> Can never cloud Thy glorious reign."

The parables of the Talents and the Pounds give another motive for looking forward with joy to the second Advent. It will be a time of reward to the diligent servant. Job tells us how the labourer "earnestly desireth the shadow," that is, watches the lengthening of the shadows as the sun goes down in the evening, knowing by this that the time of rest, refreshment, and payment is coming on. So the Christian man works on till the evening of his life, and then is ready to lie down and take his rest, and to receive the wages he has earned. So St. Paul could say, "The time of my departure is at hand; I have fought a good fight, I have finished my course, I have kept the faith; henceforth there is laid up for me a crown of righteousness, which the Lord shall give me at that day." How many like him have come to the end of life, and looked on with humble but most sure confidence to rest and reward; "Faithful unto death," they have believed in the promise of "the crown of life." One we read of said just at the last, "I never thought it was so sweet a thing to die." The venerable Polycarp, as he went forth to a martyr's death, "seemed like a bridegroom going to meet his bride," and said, "O Father of Thy beloved and blessed Son Jesus Christ; O God of all principalities and of all creation, I bless Thee that Thou hast counted me worthy of this day and this hour, to receive my portion in the number of the martyrs in the cup of Christ." Others have sung with strange sweetness just before their death. Some have seemed to see angels and departed friends, or even their Lord Himself, coming to receive their departing souls.

Ah, well may we cry, "Let me die the death of the righteous, and let my last end be like his;" for "Eye hath not seen, nor ear heard, neither have entered into the heart of man, the things which God hath prepared for them that love Him." We are not told, because we could not understand, what the home of God and His saints is. Revelation speaks only in parables, of beauty and riches. Our Lord tells us how some "Enter into the joy of their Lord;" not merely filled with joy, but plunged into a sea of all-encompassing joy, "All rapture through and through;" no human joy, but "The joy of their Lord;" and what must that be? He makes them rulers over cities in His new earth, wherein dwelleth righteousness; they are kings reigning with Him.

> "Oh what the joy and the glory must be,
> Those endless Sabbaths the blessed ones see."

If Advent tells of all this, surely the godly soul must look up and rejoice, longing for redemption, hasting unto the coming of the Lord Jesus Christ.

> "Now in the meanwhile, with hearts raised on high,
> We for that country must yearn and must sigh;
> Seeking Jerusalem, dear native land,
> Through our long exile on Babylon's strand."

But it is time we turned to more sober and practical thoughts. Mere thinking of heaven's delights will not bring us to them; reading of saints and their wonderful experience will do but little to bring us to their unspeakable joys. God's promises are glorious, His rewards are infinite, but they have to be toiled for, fought for, suffered for. Heaven is our Home, but there is a weary way between us and it yet. The crown is given only to the martyr, the wages only to him who has toiled in the sweat of his face.

Let us then turn again to the parables; one servant receives talents, another a pound; years pass, and each day of those years has seen those servants trading with their master's goods, slowly, steadily increasing them, in spite of misfortunes, disappointments, hindrances. They sow in hope, sometimes in tears, hoping against hope; they labour, they watch. By and by the harvest comes, and one reaps thirty, one sixty, one a hundred fold. Then harvest leads on to sowing again; for there is no rest till the Lord comes.

Let us notice, too, that the nobleman goes to obtain a kingdom, but he does not take his servants to help him; he does not arm them with swords, but leaves them behind each with a pound. So our Lord Christ with His own right hand gets Himself the victory; we can do nothing in His tremendous conflict; but the easy work that He sets us, that we must do. He has done the hard work Himself. He has made it possible for us to do great things for Him; He expects more of us than of the old-world saints, who knew so much less of God than we know, and who had no sacraments, and no abiding Holy Ghost. We can turn all things to gold by a touch, the touch of faith that makes common things, little things, acceptable to God; the touch of Jesus Christ, that makes our poor deeds pleasing to God.

There is a saying handed down by ancient writers, which they tell us was uttered by our Lord, though it is not recorded by the Evangelists, "Be ye good exchangers." It is the same word that is used in the parable. The banker or exchanger receives money from others, and turns it to his own advantage, so does the godly man receive his Pound from God, his life with its gifts, reason, conscience, time, and using it well as God's loan, he returns it to God with many good things added and gained. The wise banker discerns between the genuine coin and the counterfeit, the sound investment and the swindling trap; so the servant of God has an eye to distinguish between the gold of the sanctuary and the gilt of the world. There are tempting offers, but he suspects, nay, he is sure that they are deceitful and ruinous, and he is not taken in; he is a "good banker;" he lays out his time, his youth, his work, his pleasure wisely, while fools and prodigals waste their substance in riotous living, and presently are in want, and in debt. As an old Bishop said, "To give to pious uses, is to put our monies out to interest upon the security of God Himself;" or as another has said, "The hands of the poor of Christ are the safest Bank."

Even among the wise some are wiser than others; all receive the Pound, but one makes it into ten pounds, another only into five; and no doubt among the remaining seven servants, who received each a pound and of whom nothing is told us, there were other varieties of success. The great day of light will reveal many surprises, the first last, and the last first; some "In a short time fulfil a long time;" many will be surprised at the fruit of their humble labours.

There is a legend of the primitive ages, that a holy man who had retired into the desert to live alone with God, away from the world, in it but not of it, was bidden to go and seek counsel from one far holier than he, and he found him, a poor unknown working man, living in the midst of a large town with all its sins and distractions. People complain of their difficulties and hindrances; when the day of light comes, they will see how others have overcome the same or greater difficulties, and turned all to the glory of God, and their own soul's good. The healthy man turns the plainest food into nourishment and strength, the sickly man is no better for the choicest fare; it turns into evil humours, and makes him ill. It is said, "It is only a bad workman who complains of his tools."

Let this then be our Advent thought to-day; God has entrusted to each one of us His Pound, our life; let us live it for Him. Each one of us can make it honourable, useful, happy here; and when the Great Day comes there will be something to show for it, something that God will accept, something that will not pass away, but will still be ours, making us to have treasure in heaven, and to be great and joyous in the eternal kingdom of our Father.

Friday after the Fourth Sunday.

PRAYING FOR THE COMING OF CHRIST.

THE present season of the year is specially one of hope. It is the dull dark bleak time; the days have come of which we say, "We have no pleasure in them." But we look on with hope to brightness again, to sun and flowers, and longer days, and more genial temperature. We cannot live, certainly we cannot be happy, without hope. In the buoyancy of childhood we lived mostly on hope; we were so eager for the future that we scarcely gave ourselves time to enjoy the present. We were always hurrying on to the next thing, and had high hopes of it that it would be better than anything that had come before. As years passed, and experience matured, we gradually learned to rate things lower, to be less eager, to weigh and ponder and reason, rather than to act on mere impulse. But still we cherished hopes. And when old age comes, and the present has small satisfaction in it, and the future may be said scarcely to exist for us, what shall we do then? Shall we hope still? And if so, what shall we hope for? Surely as with the old age of the dying year, so with the old age of human life, we must cling to hope, as it looks on to a new era; we know that our present time is nearly past; our present destiny is nearly played out; we must look elsewhere for safe holding ground for the anchor of our hopes. This is especially the Christian spirit. It rests itself chiefly on hopes beyond this world. Christ has taught us not to make this world our home. He warns us against trusting to its tempting offers. He bids us live as strangers and travellers whose home is far away. He tells us that this world's ills are mostly incurable; He inculcates patience indeed and fulfilment of present duty, but He says that we must lay up all our treasures in Heaven, and fix our hearts there. Young and old, He will have all alike in this that they look out of themselves and beyond this soon-to-be-ended life into another life as the sphere of their hopes.

All this He does when He teaches us ever to pray, "Thy kingdom come." They are awful words to use; they cast an Advent shade across every season, every day of the year and of our lives, for we are bidden to say daily whenever we pray, " Thy kingdom come." The thought of death is awful to human nature; the thought of Judgment is yet more intolerable; to see God face to face for the first time, and then as our Judge, this is a tremendous thing. And this is not merely to be endured as an inevitable certainty, but it is to be prayed for; such is our Master's will. Does not this speak volumes respecting the Christian's calling? How it strips off unrealities and sophistries, and searches out the state of the inmost heart, and makes us already feel as if the great day had come, and we had to judge ourselves each alone face to face with God!

Nor do these words stand alone. If we will notice what Christ and His holy ones say, we shall see that the same tone runs through all. The very last recorded words of our Lord are, "Behold, I come quickly," and the inspired response is, "Even so, come, Lord Jesus." The souls of the holy dead are pictured to us crying to God,

"How long?" praying for His coming in His Kingdom. Our Lord's words are many in which He implies that His coming will necessarily elicit joy in his servants, "When these things begin to come to pass, then lift up your heads, for your redemption draweth nigh;" "I will see you again, and your heart shall rejoice." So in the Old Testament, "O show yourselves joyful before the Lord the king, for He cometh to judge the earth." So in the prayers of the Church, "We beseech Thee of Thy gracious goodness shortly to accomplish the number of Thine elect, and to hasten Thy Kingdom." It is told us of a holy man that in speaking of his age he used not to say how old he was, but that he was in such and such a year of his "exile from Paradise."

These instances are but a few out of many, where the same joy is spoken of as a matter of course with those who look for His appearing. Have we ever noticed this? Have we discerned the searching practical character of this Advent thought? It sounds unreal; there seems paradox in it; there seems contradiction between such a spirit and the timidity with which even great saints, such as St. Paul, speak of the uncertainty of their salvation. Yet there it stands; a truth not to be gainsaid, that we should rejoice at the thought of Christ's coming again, and daily pray, "Thy kingdom come." If it is unreal and impossible to us, there must be fault in ourselves.

Let us notice a few of the reasons for this prayer on the lips of the children of God. Children honour their father, and desire his exaltation and glory; "Our Father, hallowed be Thy Name, Thy kingdom come, Thy will be done in earth as it is in Heaven." There is evil rampant, there is rebellion, there is disorder in the realm of God; we cannot understand it, but we can hate it. He does not explain it, but He bids us pray for its extinction. There are misery and suffering among men, wrongs that must be against the good will of our Father in Heaven; we do not understand the reason, and He does not explain it, but He bids us pray, "Thy kingdom come." The day of Judgment will be awful; it will bring on the doom of sinners; but it is the will of God, and we acquiesce in that will. The day of Judgment will bring rest and joy to the redeemed; in their joy the Saviour will see of the travail of His soul and be satisfied, and so we pray "Thy kingdom come." The dead in Christ are waiting and longing for the day; all those who love God and Christ long to see Him as He is face to face, for love never rests satisfied with absence. Memory is sweet, but it is the presence, not the mere memory, of loved ones that we desire; and

"If memory sometimes at our spell
Refuse to speak, or speak amiss,
We shall not need her where we dwell,
Ever in sight of all our bliss."

These many years God's children have clung to Him in spirit, drawn near to Him in the way He has bidden them, the only possible way as yet, in prayer, in Holy Communion; they have cleansed themselves continually from every stain of sin, bathed in the Precious Blood, prepared themselves for this very thing, shall they not then rejoice when at last it comes in very deed? All the ills they groan under they expect His coming will drive away; all the darkness that may be felt in their souls the brightness of His coming will dissipate; they are weary with fighting, He will bring rest and victory; they weep as captives by the waters of Babylon, shall they not look on to the promised time when there shall be a shout in Heaven, "Babylon the great is fallen, and the kingdoms of this world are become the kingdom of our God and of His Christ, and He shall reign for ever and ever"?

> "The distant landscape draws not nigh
> For all our gazing; but the soul,
> That upward looks, may still descry
> Nearer, each day, the brightening goal."

"Thy kingdom come;" "The kingdom of heaven is at hand;" "Thy will be done;" "Prepare to meet thy God;" How shall we prepare? What is His will? "The kingdom of God is within you." Advent is nearly over, Christmas is at hand; let us prepare to meet our Judge by meeting now our Saviour; let us come to Bethlehem, and rejoice, so shall we rejoice also when He cometh in majesty who now comes in great humility. The great feast of the marriage of the King's Son will soon be proclaimed, let us betake ourselves to His birthday feast now, and so be welcomed at that greater gathering, when He Himself will come in to see His guests. There shall be a severing at the Great Day of those who love His appearing from those who cry ever to Him, "Depart from me;" let us see that we are with Him and His on Christmas day; not with those who depart and turn their backs upon Him, but with those who draw near in spite of fear, in spite of deep sighs over sins and infirmities; who fear to come, but who fear more to stay away. "Thy kingdom come," cries the loving heart; "Come unto Me," says the Lord that bought thee. Each cries to the other, "Come;" surely there must one day be a joyful meeting, a blissful eternal union.

Christmas Eve.

GOING TO BETHLEHEM.

ALL over the world men's thoughts to-day are turning to Bethlehem. Among the souls of God's faithful, resting from their labours, waiting for us, waiting for the second Advent, the thoughts of many hearts are bending thither, in thankful, loving memory. And doubt we not that that "multitude of the heavenly host," who as at this time brought heaven's songs to earth, remember Bethlehem to-day, and in thought turn thither? And does not He go again in spirit to Bethlehem, Who as at this time went there in great humility and in our flesh? And we, shall not we too join this throng of spirits, unrestrained by the bonds of the flesh, not let and hindered by distance, or lack of time, or pressure of other duties, shall not we, by the power of will and the operation of our free spirits, "Go now even unto Bethlehem?"

But with whom shall we go? At this time, more than 1800 years ago, these words were said and acted upon by many different persons. There were Cæsar's tax-gatherers, they went to Bethlehem on business and for their own interests; there was money to be collected there, and these publicans knew how to get profit to themselves out of the taxes that passed through their hands. Shall we go to Bethlehem with these, and with their motives and ideas? Better not; Bethlehem is after all but a poor little place; be as hard and unscrupulous and exacting as they may, these tax-gatherers will not get much for themselves, when they have collected all that is due from that small mountain village. If we want to get on in the world and sail with the stream, if we want to make money, and do well for ourselves, and get the world's good things, we had better leave such places as Bethlehem alone. Great, rich, beautiful, pleasure-loving Babylon is the city for us; or luxurious Sodom, or the ancient and marvellous cities of Egypt, or gossiping philosophical Athens, with its "Unknown God;" or Tyre, with its merchant princes; these places are more to our taste; better far go to one or the other of them.

But there is another who wants to go to Bethlehem; shall we go with him? The great Herod says he wishes to go there, and worship the new-born King. But he intends to take an executioner with him, and as soon as he finds Jesus, he will order the executioner to tear Him from His Mother's arms, and murder Him. Shall we go in company with Herod to Bethlehem? There are some ready to go with him; "They give good words with their mouth, but curse with their heart." Jesus is still actually hated by not a few. He would be murdered over again, if He were now to come into the world, if some had their way. There is Calvary in many a man and woman's heart at this moment, and there Jesus is put to death. There is the spirit of Herod, lurking, and acting its will, as far as it can in the little world, within many a one, little suspected; it sharpens a sword and sheds innocent blood in the endeavour to rid itself of its rival, its enemy, the disturber of its peace, Jesus.

Let us see the others who are on their way to Bethlehem. There is a poor young woman of Nazareth, married not yet twelve months, herself still almost a child, who has been walking along mountain paths with her husband to-day to go to Bethlehem. The decree of the Emperor compelled her to go, to be taxed at her husband's native town, but a Greater than he had ordered this ages before, and made all things work to bring it to pass. Some time ago she had said, "Be it unto me according to Thy word," and the spirit of those words had ever been the guide of her life. Humble, sweet obedience, perfect devotion to the will of God, self-abnegation and sacrifice, simple trusting faith, these are the thoughts of her heart as she goes to Bethlehem, bearing in her bosom her Creator, her Saviour, her God, the Wonderful, the eternal Jehovah. Hovering over and about her, preceding, following, surrounding her, are hosts of lovely, glorious angels, watching, guarding, directing her steps, and worshipping the while, and adoring Him whom she bears within her. These too are going to Bethlehem; soon to burst out with heaven's songs even here upon earth, "Glory to God in the highest."

Then there were those few poor shepherds, they too went to Bethlehem; in simple faith, with small store of wisdom, with no learning, poor, ignorant, unknown peasants. Lastly, in contrast with these, the Wise Men from the far distant East, kings, it is said, with wealth and circumstance and many retainers, themselves learned, great, rich, holding intercourse with none less than Herod himself, as kings should consort with kings; these came with much expense, much fatigue, from a very far country; they came to lay their crowns at the feet of the new-born King, and as kings to present royal gifts to the King of kings.

Such then is the company offered us; such are they who say, "Let us now go even unto Bethlehem." Mary and Joseph, the holy Angels, the poor Shepherds, the Wise Men from the East. If we have decided that with Herod and Cæsar's publicans we will not go, then with which of those shall we find ourselves most at home? If we are poor and unlearned, the Shepherds will gladly have us with them. If we are rich and well educated, the Wise Men from the East will be congenial companions. In one or other of these companies every one of us can find sympathy, if only we have with them the same object.

Why should we go to Bethlehem? To greet, to worship Jesus, to welcome a Saviour who can free us from sin, who can open heaven to us, and lead us thither our true home, who can promise us peace on earth in the midst of all the disquieting weary troubles of this life, and who can tell us of that better land where trouble comes not. Yes, "Let us go now even unto Bethlehem." This is what we all want; a Saviour from our sins.

When we are come to Bethlehem, what shall we see? A little Babe lying in a manger. It is the great God humbled so low, for us humbled thus, not for our salvation only, but for our example; for we too must humble ourselves and become as this little Child. This is the great conversion, to become as a little child. This is the first lesson that stands at the beginning of the Church's year; and it is the key-note of all that follows; upon this all is built as upon a foundation; every high thing must be brought low, before Christ can be formed in us. Pride of will, pride of intellect, pride of independence, pride of high place and consideration, pride of envied possession. Oh what fruitful sources of sin and misery are all these? Let us go to Bethlehem to pull them down; let us lay them down at the Manger, where God Almighty is lying humbled, a little helpless Child, sharing with the dumb beasts the poor shelter of a stable. Let us keep all this, like the blessed Mother, and ponder it in our hearts, and we shall learn wondrous lessons of divine wisdom, clean contrary to the world's maxims and principles, but true and real and lasting, tried by many before us, and found so to be in the rough troubled sea of life, and in the dark terror-strewn valley of death.

The world is full of cries, full of voices, full of remedies for the evils of humanity. There are many schemes, many teachers, many theories, but "Let us go even unto Bethlehem." They tell us that Christianity has had its day; that it is falling before the march of intellect; that it is falling through the divisions and wranglings of sects; but "Let us go even unto Bethlehem." Faith and love are wonderfully quickened there, and those who are going to the same end, are likely by this to become of one heart and of one mind. Yes, be this our way; we may go halting, doubting, stopping, turning aside, turning back, falling sometimes, idly sleeping sometimes, wasting the day's best hours, sometimes more than half persuaded to give up our quest, and turn to some other greater, or more joyous, or more learned, or more luxurious city, or one nearer and easier to reach, or one that seems more popular with others, or more congenial to our own tastes and fancies; there are many such; but still, "Let us go even unto Bethlehem." This, the one city for us; this, after all and in spite of all, our aim and end; for there is Jesus, our Lord, our Saviour, our God; and where He is, there is the soul's rest, and peace, and joy; there, and there only, its Home.

Christmas Day.

JESUS OUR BROTHER.

WHEN Jacob was told that his dear son Joseph, whom he had long mourned as dead, was alive, that he was a great man in honour and power, that he had not forgotten his old father, but still loved him as dearly as ever, that he had sent for him to come to him, to be cared for and cherished, in that time of famine and scarceness, it was too much for him, he could not believe it. So no doubt Joseph's brothers were incredulous, when the great man before whom they trembled, who had power of life and death, and who seemed to have taken an unreasonable prejudice against them, and had already made them suffer sharply, when he said to them, "I am Joseph, your brother." They had last seen him a poor wailing beseeching lad, half naked, with his hands tied, being led off by the hard dealers who had bought him for a slave. People are very apt to forget that boys, whom they have not seen for years, have grown up in the meantime into men. That handsome man sitting in state, robed, attended, obeyed, where was the smallest resemblance in him to their brother Joseph? Yet as they "came near," that subtle thing, family likeness, betrayed itself. Hitherto they had been kept at a respectful distance from the great man; now as they stand close to him, Joseph's eyes are there under the regal head-dress; Joseph's face seems to come back with a flash; Joseph's voice with its unmistakeable tones convinces their ears. For a man's features, his personal peculiarities, belong to him alone; and so the banker, with all his precautions and safeguards, has to trust at last to the individual characteristics of his client's signature. That marvellous thing, individuality, is proof positive; their brother is there; incredible, inexplicable as it may be. The great man, the terrible man in authority, the man who is so far above them, the man who can do what he will with them, all this is done away; Joseph reassures them over and over again, and puts them at their ease with the repeated announcement, which is at once an argument, a reason, and a final conclusion, "I am your Brother."

Are we not reminded of this touching episode to-day? What does the great God say to us this Christmas day from the cradle at Bethlehem but the same wondrous words, "I am your Brother"? It would have been quite incredible, but that Joseph's story and many another had prepared us for it. If there was a tremendous distance between the mighty governor of Egypt, and these poor shepherds in a strange land, asking to be allowed to buy a little corn, which they could get nowhere else to save them from starvation, what is the distance between the great God and us? In the old world the wise had imagined God infinitely removed from poor mortals. He might exist in the plenitude of His majesty, in the resistless realm of His power, in His happiness that He would let none disturb; but no mortal could find Him. He had hemmed Himself in, and surrounded His domains to far off limits with impassable bounds, with hosts of guards and powerful inferiors, who would be inexorable to prayer, and who would ward off all possible intrusion; and to these beings were committed, as they believed, all human affairs, and their passion, or caprice, or indifference, made wild work with human hopes and fears and sorrows. The favoured few, kings, nobles, learned men, might perhaps be noticed and cared for, but the mass of humanity, the poor, the suffering, the sick, the child, the woman; individuals with their heart aches, their poor little troubles known only to themselves, their yearnings after a friend, a father, a brother, up above among higher, nobler beings than any earthly kinship could realize, these were doomed to hopeless disappointment; there was no comfort in religion for them. They must grovel in terror of malignant deities; they must propitiate their cruel propensities with painful and degrading rites and offerings. Oh, this Christmas day let us remember all this; and shall we not rejoice, and praise, and thank God?

It was doubtless man's own fault that He had so lost the knowledge of God; but the ignorance must have been painful and most miserable. This we are spared; we know what God is. The speechless Babe, that holds out His little arms to us from a human Mother's embrace, says with an eloquence that no words could equal, "I am your Brother; come near to me, I pray you." Oh the wondrous mercy, the loving tenderness of God! How can any resist it? How can any argue against it? How can men go back again of their own free will to the old despairing darkness, now that this light has shined from the Manger at Bethlehem, now that these good tidings have been proclaimed which were so longed for, so sorely needed?

Some in the old world had dreamed of celestial beings coming down among men, and becoming leaders and divinities among them, but who had ever imagined the humiliations of Bethlehem? Who had dared to hope that God would be with us thus? If He had sent some exalted angelic being to dwell among us, to tell us what God is, to stoop as the great and pure only can, to sympathize with poor inferior creatures in their sorrows and troubles; it would have been a blessed revelation, a most comforting, grateful visitation of God. If He had come Himself in some spiritualised form, and had manifested Himself sometimes, in one place, at rare and far apart occasions, and told us some of the truths we so longed to know; this would have been more than men had hoped for. But what is this to the Christmas Day truth? What can we do but rejoice and adore, worship and give thanks, wonder and love?

"Come near to me, I pray you; I am your Brother." God has become Man, one of our race; with a human body, a human mind, with human affections, feelings, sensibilities, sympathies. He has lived in this world as we live to-day, eating, working, sleeping, sorrowing, rejoicing. He had friends; life was sweet to Him, as to us; death was dreaded, but endured. There is nothing that happens to us, nothing that we feel, but He can understand it, sympathize with it; not because He is God and knows all things, but because He was and is Man, and nothing human is alien to Him.

The great man may be a friend of the poor man, but God has made Himself our Brother; one of the great family of the human race. Joseph in his greatness encouraged his brothers to "come near" to him, but God has done more. He Himself has "come near" to us. The step is His; such is His good will towards men; towards each one of us in our several needs. Glory be to God, thanks be to God, this day and for ever, for this miracle of love! He takes our love by storm, and carries us away by the torrent of His goodness.

But even this is not all. He might have come as a Man, in the full plenitude of life's best years; He might have come in power, wisdom, greatness, teaching God's truth in majestic circumstance, raised far above all men, exempt from all suffering, all humiliations, and presently returning to the Right Hand of God. But He did none of this. He began as we begin in helpless infancy; He trusted Himself in helplessness to a woman's tenderness, a mother's love. He stooped to poverty; He suffered; He was despised, ill-treated; He remained ignorant of the delights of learning; He never had access to the beautiful, the magnificent; wedded love was not His; His life was full of sorrows; and He made proof at last of that dreadful experience, death. The humiliation of Bethlehem was but the key-note of His whole life. Life is full of trouble; in this He was our Brother. Life has many joys; life is different to different men, different to each at different times, but it is in its lowest depths that a helping hand is needed; it is the suffering, the sad, the unfortunate, who need a helper; "A brother is born for adversity," and He is our Brother.

Oh glorious, wondrous, blessed truth! Oh most marvellous revelation! The more we think of it, the more wonderful, inexplicable, it seems. It takes away our breath, and wraps us in silent worship. "Oh come let us adore Him." What else can we do? Let our heart's yearning instinct have its way, and it will lead us to Bethlehem, and prostrate us there, the willing servants, the faithful believers, the passionate lovers of Jesus. "Come near to me, I pray you," He says, that is all; and that is enough. If we will but do that, all is done; we are His evermore, and He is ours. Is it not because men stand afar off, reasoning, questioning, carping, that they do not believe? Is it not because they put sins between Him and their souls? The world's passing toys, the sloth, the lusts, the poor degrading animal indulgences, the little things of the moment, the men of each day's trivial events, these keep souls afar off, and so God is not known, not loved, not trusted. Oh that all would just take Him at His word, and "Come near" to Him, so should they find rest, hope, peace, joy!

St. Stephen.

THE TWO GREAT MOTHERS.

WHEN Cain was born, we are told that Eve exclaimed, "I have gotten a man from the Lord." How much is implied in these words. For the first time Eve knew that wonderful mystery, the birth of a child. To us it is so common an event that we cease to think how very wonderful it is. But to her it was all new, all strange. This living, breathing, beautiful little creature she accepted at once as "from the Lord." God's work, God's gift. Her own flesh and blood, her own likeness, her heart yearned and rejoiced over it; a new delight entered into her and possessed her, such as none but a mother's heart can know. She could gaze upon the little thing with never-wearied, ever-satisfied love; she found fresh delight in her treasure every day; every care that it demanded seemed but to make her love it more, and rejoice more deeply in the wealth of its possession.

But there was another thought which she had, which these words teach us. She had disobeyed God, and seduced her husband to disobedience; she had ruined him and the world; she had forfeited Paradise. There was a dark pall ever between her heart and the joy of God's countenance. They were exiles, those two sinners, she and her husband; they remembered the blessedness of Eden, the society of God there, and the glorious liberty and lightness and overflowing happiness of a pure, sinless heart. The deep, awful loss of this settled upon them as soon as they sinned, and ever since the curse had been working and developing itself. They saw it, and felt it growing and spreading around them and within them, till it seemed too much to bear, too dreadful a thing to live on thus; remorse and apprehension their constant companions. One only bright spot remained to them, one star of hope among the black, threatening clouds. When the curse had been laid upon them, there was one mysterious word of mercy. As they listened with bowed heads and shame-reddened faces to the dreadful sentence, there was a promise, only half heard in their confusion, not well understood till afterwards, but now stored up in their souls as their best treasure; the promise of a Son who should crush the serpent's head, and undo the evil he had done to them. And now a son was born, was not the promise fulfilled? Was not this "The man from the Lord"? It had been weary waiting so long, but now they "remembered no more the anguish, for joy that a man, the man, was born into the world." "I have gotten a man from the Lord," or, as some read it, "I have gotten a man, the Lord." Yes, here was a treasure indeed; and so they called him Cain, "a Possession," their one precious thing, a gift from God, worthy of the Giver, the centre of all their hopes.

Alas! we know it was not so to be. God's time had not yet come. If the need was great then, it must be seen to be greater yet before the Saviour would come; evil must grow and abound; good men must suffer and wait, and be sick at heart with waiting and hope deferred, and die without receiving the promise. Men must trust God with what was quite beyond their understanding, the victory of evil, the ruin of souls which we should have said had better never been born. And more; this desire of their eyes must pierce his parents' heart through with many sorrows; a rebel, a murderer, an outcast, this he was to be; and he who was born next, and whom they valued so lightly that they called him Abel, that is " Vanity;" he was to be the type of the coming Saviour, and the first fruits of His Atonement. So foolish were they and ignorant; so little did they understand God's ways and purposes.

But now to-day the old words come up again, for Bible words have a way of repeating themselves; they seem dead and done with, but new circumstances give them new life and meaning; heaven and earth pass away, but God's words pass not away, but abide and live for ever. To-day again it is true, " We have gotten a man from the Lord;" nay, now certainly, " a Man, the Lord." Now the words are true in all their fulness. He is come of whom they were spoken at first in mistaken, premature desire, He who should bruise the serpent's head, and undo the curse, and open again the gate of Paradise, and reconcile man to God.

The early Christian writers, who were almost contemporary with the Apostles, delight to dwell on the analogies and contrasts between that woman who brought sin into the world and her whom all generations call Blessed. We cannot rightly understand the record of the Fall without referring to the last of the Apostles. Genesis is best explained by Revelation. It is not till we come to those closing pages of God's Word that we are distinctly told that the Serpent was Satan, although it had been assumed often before. In the last pages of inspiration, as in the first, there is the woman with her child, and the serpent attacking them; only in Genesis the serpent seems to prevail, while in Revelation he is vanquished, crushed and destroyed for ever. So Justin, a writer of the first century, compares the Virgin Eve conceiving the evil word of the serpent, with the Virgin Mother of our Lord conceiving the eternal Word, breathed forth upon her by the Holy Ghost. Other writers all through the subsequent ages dwell with devout pleasure upon the evident similarity, and the blessed contrast, in the positions of the two great mothers in the history of mankind, the one the mother of woe and cursing, the other the mother of blessing and salvation.

But it pleased God to work in mystery. This second better mother must have rejoiced indeed as on this day. None can conceive the depth and purity of her joy. God had not only ordained her to inconceivable dignity, but had made her fit for that dignity. For nine months God Almighty, the Creator of the world, had dwelt in her bosom; of her substance His Human Body was formed; her face was repeated in His Face, as sons are like their mothers. The Body in which He lived and suffered, the Body which He gave and gives spiritually to be the food of the faithful for ever, the Body He took to heaven, which is now adored by the unnumbered hosts who dwell there, which will be seen coming in the clouds of heaven, and which all men will see upon the great white Throne on the Judgment day, this Body was bone of her bone and flesh of her flesh; God was her Son, her Babe, hers alone. Can we over-rate her dignity? Can we conceive her joy? And yet the sword soon pierced her bosom. The Magnificat soon changes into a minor wail at the Cross, with no words that are recorded; for her sorrow was too deep for words.

But even now there is a look of the old disappointment in the life-work of this much-desired Son. The world rejected Him and still rejects Him; and the Church, which should be so pure and glorious and beneficent, what an aspect does it present to loving devout earnest eyes this Christmas Day!

But we must not dwell on this to-day. It is a day of gladness, not of sorrow; of hope, not of foreboding; of thankfulness and trust, not of querulous, faithless despondency. For what does all this teach us but to wait and hope? Eve was wrong, impatient. Four thousand years went by before her words came really true. This is God's way. We must wait and hope; we have blessings already; we "drink of the brook in the way," but we still turn our eyes onward and upward. Christmas Day is blessed, but we are not satisfied; we know there are better things to come. We rejoice to-day in God our Saviour, but some of the shadow that lowered over Eve's joy hangs over us too. Only let us not fall into her mistake, but rather follow the example of her who "kept all God's words and pondered them in her heart;" waiting, hoping, trusting. There are better things to come. To-day's gladness is a sure token of this; "He that letteth will let, till he be taken out of the way," and then the long-desired Redeemer will come, and take His own, and conquer, and reign: and truth shall drive away falsehood; and peace shall reign instead of war; and love shall bow all loving hearts to its gentle dominion. Other generations of God's servants have waited and hoped before us, and died leaning all their weight upon their faith; to this too we are called; already we seem to see a gleam of light in the East; surely He comes quickly. Even so, come, Lord Jesus.

St. John.

MEETING THE JUDGE AT BETHLEHEM.

WHEN a man's mind is full of some particular thought, everything he says and does feels its influence. A joy, a sorrow, a plan, an expectation, tinges with its own tone all that happens to a man. Now it is the same with the Bible. The Incarnation of the Son of God was from the beginning in the mind of God; holy men of old wrote as they were moved by the Holy Ghost; they recorded certain events; they rescued from oblivion the names and passing words and acts of seemingly insignificant men; and the meaning of all they wrote is found in one word, Christ. There is much that is infinitely valuable in the Old Testament; it is profitable for many things; but under everything else there lies the thought of Christ. The annals of great nations, the memory of noble deeds, the names of great men, are gone, utterly lost; but certain persons, certain events, certain words, in the annals of a small and unimportant people, that once had its home at the eastern end of the Mediterranean Sea, these have been wonderfully recorded, and still more wonderfully preserved, because they are full of Christ; and these are handed down to us for our learning. The people whose they were understand them not; like the vessel that holds the precious wine, like the animal that generates and protects and hides the beautiful pearl, the Jew held fast the

Word of God, but it is for us to open, to appreciate, to be blessed by its deep and glorious mysteries. Just as in families we detect a feature, an inflection of the voice, a trick of doing something; just as in a piece of music we catch a trace of the theme; just as in a mass of flowers we detect the powerful scent of some one that the rest cannot smother; so the devout Christian discovers Christ his Lord in almost every page of the Old Testament, often in most unlikely places, and veiled under strange disguises; and proves for himself the truth of those words of His, that the Old Testament Scriptures testify of Him.

Take, for example, that incident in the life of Samuel, when, ordered by the command of God, he went to Bethlehem to anoint David King. We read, "Samuel came to Bethlehem; and the elders of the town trembled at his coming, and said, Comest thou peaceably? and he said, Peaceably: I am come to sacrifice unto the Lord; sanctify yourselves, and come with me to the sacrifice." See now these words, how full they are of Christ, what lessons they teach us, fit for Christmas tide. Samuel the Judge comes to Bethlehem, and at once the people are afraid; he was the supreme ruler of Israel, his word was law; God heard his prayer, and punished those whom he denounced. Bethlehem was a small place, and not used to the visits of great men; the consciences of the elders told them of many a cause for complaint, many a just ground for punishment; and so they go to meet their Judge not without fear and apprehension; and they are relieved indeed when they hear that he comes not for vengeance, but to call them to a sacrifice. "A guilty conscience makes cowards of us all." Sin makes men afraid of God; Adam hid himself, and every sinful and impenitent, and therefore unpardoned child of Adam, still does the same.

"Depart from me, O God, let me hide from God;" these are the sinner's thoughts. All through the Bible there are warnings of judgment to come, the sure word that God will not always be out of sight, nor man left to go his own way, but that God and man will come face to face again, and that there will be a reckoning and a retribution. So when the cry passes from mouth to mouth, "God has come, the Judge is here," the inevitable thought is terror; the hills tremble at His presence, men's hearts fail them for fear.

Welcome then Christmas-tide; thrice welcome the angel's message. Men say fearfully, "Comest thou peaceably?" And the answer is "Peaceably, with good-will towards men." The Judge has come suddenly to Bethlehem; but oh how strangely! He has not visited men in wrath, nor vexed them in His sore displeasure; but He hath visited us in great humility, peaceably, the Prince of peace, with peace to men of good-will. The Judge has come, but the sword of justice is not seen. God has come, but there is nothing to terrify us. We had read, "Who may abide the day of His coming?" We had read that men should call upon the rocks to fall upon them and hide them from the face of God; we go to Bethlehem trembling, and saying, "Comest Thou peaceably?" And the answer is the wail of an Infant that lies helpless, and stretches out His arms to us, as if to claim our protection! All is reversed; the Creator is subject to His creature, to prove His love. God has put Himself into our power. No words could say so much as that marvellous act; a speechless Babe that cannot even frame a word to declare its own helplessness. Oh infinite love of God! Oh condescending love of God! Oh most eloquent silence of that Infant mouth! No human preacher's, no angel's words can speak like that, and tell of "Peace on earth, good will towards men."

Acts of love, how much more compelling are they even than sweetest words! Go look at some new-born babe; see what it is; see what it needs; and then remember that as at this time Almighty God became a Babe just like that, to prove to the world His good-will to men! Nay, take it to thyself, O soul, that would know what thy God is to thee. Put away hard thoughts, doubting thoughts, questions, difficulties; there is much that none can ever understand of God and His ways, but this at least is clear; this all can understand; from no necessity but only from pitying love of thee, O soul, whom thy sins have ruined, thy God became a little Child, as at this time! Like Mary, keep this one most marvellous, most blessed truth, and ponder it in thy heart. That little Child is set in our midst as our Teacher, to teach us what we should be, but much more to teach us what our God is. "He that hath seen the Son, hath seen the Father." This is our God; prophets said He was loving, but men for very fear would not believe it. He sent messages, He did deeds of love, He gave gifts, He refrained from judgment, but still men shrank away from Him in fear; and now He has flung Himself at our feet, an abject human Babe, to compel us to trust Him, to love Him. Down on thy knees, O man; cover thy face, shut out the world; let thy heart gaze upon that sight; if that will not make thee love and trust God, what more can He do?

And yet there is more; "They said, Comest thou peaceably? and he said, Peaceably; I am come to sacrifice unto the Lord." Sacrifice! What sacrifice can there be more than we see in the stable of Bethlehem? What remains yet for sacrifice when God has already emptied Himself? The Infinite has become finite, the Almighty weak, the Lord of all dependent upon one of His creatures, just exactly as your new-born babe, O woman, is now dependent upon you. What imagination could have thought of this? Who shall imagine another sacrifice yet? And yet there was one then in the mind of God. That human Body was prepared that it might be offered up; that human Life was commenced that it might end in the Sacrifice of the Cross.

Oh hard, dull, sinful heart of man, hast thou been gazing all this time upon the Babe at Bethlehem, upon God incarnate for thee, and yet art not moved? Then there is yet one more picture, Christ upon His Cross, thy Saviour sacrificing Himself for thee, thy God dying for thee, bleeding, suffering even to the death for thee, because He loved thee, that He might save thee, that He might teach thee, compel thee to love Him.

Now indeed God can do no more; if such love will not convert men, God Himself knows nothing more powerful; if the unreserved sacrifices of boundless love will not turn men's hearts to their loving God, then they must go their own way; but who will dare to say that the lost soul has any to blame but itself? Curse thyself, O lost one, but thou canst not curse God; none will believe thee; all would cry, Shame on thee; heaven and earth; men and angels; yea, hell itself.

What must we do then? What must we do for whom so much has been done? The Old Testament story tells us, "Sanctify yourselves, and come with me to the sacrifice." "Come with me." The one thought of the lost unpardoned soul, whether in this world or in hell, is to get away from God. The soul that is pardoned, justified, sanctified, desires to draw near to God; love draws it on, for love is restless in absence. See then the devout soul, with eye fixed upon God, following ever the lead of Christ. The world flings its dirt upon it; it sanctifies itself, and is clean, and goes on its way. The flesh rebels, the soul's garment shows the spot instantly; but it sanctifies itself; it reaches its hand to the never-distant, never-failing fountain of the Precious Blood, and it is clean again, and goes on rejoicing. The devil tempts, sin is conceived, but ere it comes to the birth, it is crushed out by confession; pardon is obtained, the soul is sanctified, and goes on its way with its Lord.

"Come with me." This is the secret guide of the soul's life; it is always with Christ; and so is always safe. Nor is that quite all, for it stands, "Come with me to the sacrifice." There is sympathy between Christ and the sanctified soul; mutual sacrifice is the surest proof of real love. The life of Christ was a life of sacrifice, and so is the Christian's life. The Cross was ever in His mind. Even in His Transfiguration, when Moses and Elias talked with Him in His glory, they could talk of nothing but His coming Sacrifice on the Cross. And what does He say of His disciples? "Gather my saints together unto me, those that have made a covenant with me with sacrifice." Why are these martyrs' days clustered round His birthday, but to teach who they are that follow Him? Would we know whether we are on Christ's side, following Him as sanctified souls? Then let us see whether this sure proof of love is found in us, not now and then, not as a spasmodic exceptional thing, but as a habit. Is our life a life of sacrifice, willing sacrifice, for Him who sacrificed Himself wholly for us? "Sanctify yourselves, and come with me to the sacrifice." He that would get the benefit of the Sacrifice of the Cross, must himself bear his own cross, and follow his Lord daily.

There are other voices besides that of Christ. On every side there is the call in our ears, "Come with me." All sorts of inducements are held out. "Come with me," cries one, "be free; let none hamper the liberty of thy reason; come with me, and believe only what thou canst understand and prove." "Come with me, and make money," says another; "money will buy all this world's best. Come with me, and enjoy yourself, while youth and health last. Come with me, just this once, only for a little while, and you can soon go back again." "Come with me," shouts one; "Come with me," whispers another. "Come with me, come with me;" all our life long the voices are round us, but there is one still small voice in midst of the din, that we cannot but hear; and it says only, "Come with me to the sacrifice." At Advent it begins; we hear it when we visit the Babe at Bethlehem; all through Lent it is very importunate; it varies through feast and fast, on Saints' days and Sundays, in youth, and middle life, and age; in great things seldom, in small things daily; almost hourly it is heard, and men are dividing themselves already as they hear and obey, or disobey and disregard, till they almost cease to hear the voice at all; and life passes, and probation ends, and the last day comes for each; and they who have heard and obeyed it, hear it still, as they enter the dark valley; and as all sounds of earth fade away into silence, and the spirit slowly dissects itself from the close and intricate union with the body, and finds itself alone in a new world, and sorely needs a guide; oh the rest and the joy to hear still the well-known voice, "Come with Me."

Holy Innocents.

THE DOMINION OF THE LITTLE CHILD.

THERE are greater days, greater festivals of the Church, than Christmas Day, and yet there is no day so well beloved, so generally observed by us English as that blessed day. Its very name is wrapped up with all that is English. Those even who have lost the bright heavenly radiance that the Church alone can give to the festival, nevertheless share with us our earthly and human joy, and in that lower sense keep Christmas. Even this is well; for as on that day our common Lord came into our world in the form of man, and nothing human is henceforth indifferent to Him. He is one of us; He knows us and our nature and our world, not only as the Maker of all, but because He has in His own person shared in the experience of all. He went to the very bottom of the human family; He entered it at its lowest, weakest estate, that He might have sympathy with it in all its relations. He came as a Child that He might grow up through all the years of life till its maturity. He came poor, lowly, and obscure, that what is least esteemed by the world might first feel His sanctifying touch, and then all the rest be blessed by Him. "Blessed be the Lord God, for He hath visited and redeemed His people."

The Desire of all nations has come. Wise men and

poets of old spoke of and longed for this. Just as many who have lost the spiritual meaning of the Festival, which the Church alone understands, yet keep Christmas and cling to it with blind affection, so in old time the world which had lost the true and full knowledge of God, yet clung desperately to the hope of a coming Saviour, and never quite lost this one blessed truth of the primeval revelation. Go to Greece and Rome, to Egypt, Persia, India, everywhere there are reminiscences, faint and distorted indeed, but still there they are, of the past eventful history of man; everywhere there is the dim vague hope of a Saviour and of restoration. In heathen poets may be found words singularly like the mystic promises of Isaiah, telling of the revival of the primitive golden age, the freeing of all creation from curse and disorder, and its happy union again with man, its acknowledged lord. All thoughtful minds could see that creation groaned and travailed under some unfitting burden; all hoped that the goodness of God would one day lift off that burden, and make nature free and happy and perfect. We, who have the new revelation of God, we hope this same hope yet more earnestly, more reasonably. This season's great and wonderful blessing gives us ground for hope, for He who hath given us His only Son, shall He not with Him freely give us all things? All through the Bible there are promises which are not yet fulfilled, mysterious like the promises which have been fulfilled, like them not to be fully understood till the fulfilment is before our eyes; already fulfilled partially perhaps, in one sense, in several senses successively, yet still waiting the full and final realizing in God's own time.

In the record of man's original innocence there is special mention of his dominion over the lower orders of creation;

whatever their nature may have been, the fear and dread of man was upon them, and they came and went at his word. But because we do not fully know what was man's original relation to the beasts of the field, we cannot fully know the meaning of those mystic words of Isaiah, "The wolf shall dwell with the lamb, and the leopard shall lie down with the kid, and the calf, and the young lion, and the fatling together; and a little child shall lead them." They seem to indicate the restoration of Paradise; man ruling, restraining, harmonising the animals, however diverse their nature.

It has been noticed, by more than one thoughtful observer, that children are not naturally afraid of animals; unless they are taught to fear them, they trust them, love them, and when animals fear them, and will not be friendly with them, or even hurt them, their surprise, disappointment, and distress are keen and bitter. In the Bible we may see many dim foreshadowings that are full of meaning; Noah's dove, Balaam's ass, Elijah's ravens, Elisha's bears, to say nothing of the miracles that overruled inanimate nature; till we come to Christ; then we find in Him the new Adam, Lord of nature, and bowing it to His will; entering upon His work in the wilderness "with the wild beasts;" having power over all the realm of nature, and giving that power over beasts and serpents to His Apostles; a power that has been exercised by some of God's saints in all ages; and the end promised to be perfect subjection of all things under His feet, in a new heaven and a new earth, wherein dwelleth righteousness.

There may be a previous fulfilment of this, as of almost all great promises, and our present blessed commemoration gives us the clue to trace out already the realisation of this mystic prophecy of the subjection of the strong to the

o.

weak, the cruel and violent to the meek and gentle. If we look out into the world, and take in at a glance the broad characteristics of the whole animate creation, with man at its head, we see that there is a studied unity of plan; how it is impossible to give any reason for much that we find, except this, that God worked upon one ideal model, and that man was the ultimate aim and completion of the great work.

There is another sense in which we may understand this promise. Man has much in common with the lower animals, and fallen, sinful man very much in common with the wild beasts. The old classic writers notice this, and liken the passions of men to the cruel instincts of the lion, the serpent, and other terrible creatures, and say that every human vice has its counterpart in the animal kingdom. Scripture is full of such allusions. Not only those specially typical beasts, the lion and the serpent, but horse and mule, ox and ass, sheep and goat, dove and ant, all are spoken of in the Bible as possessing characteristics that are seen also in mankind.

What then does Isaiah say to us? What mean these mystic words about wolf and leopard and lion, and further on the bear, the asp, and the cockatrice, all subdued, all tamed, all feeding quietly together, with lamb and kid, calf and ox? Why the mention of this "Little Child," who rules and guides, and holds all in subjection? In Paradise Adam ruled, but he was in man's full age and majesty; why should the new Adam in the new Paradise be otherwise, and be not a man but a little child? Doubtless Isaiah, when he was moved to utter these words, wondered what the Spirit of God did testify by his mouth; doubtless those who heard and read and pondered on his prophecy wondered, and marvelled, and were perplexed at the tone of the prophecy, so different from their ideas of Messiah and His majesty. But we Christians this blessed Christmas-tide know it all; we know who this little Child is; we know that our King has come, but come meek and lowly, a Babe, Son of Mary. We read the prophecy, "Thou shalt go upon the lion and the adder, the young lion and the dragon shalt Thou tread under Thy feet." We see the Lord sending forth His disciples "as sheep among wolves," poor, unsupported, yet with "power over serpents, and all the power of the enemy." We turn to the New Testament, and see Saul making havock of the Church, " in the morning ravening like a wolf," in the evening a lamb for gentleness, an ox for labour; a disciple, an apostle, a martyr of the " Holy Child Jesus." We turn back the page of history, and see the might of Rome, compared by prophets to the ravening of a wild beast; subdued to the dominion of the Babe of Bethlehem. We read on, and we learn how Europe was desolated by wild tribes, so rude and fierce that they were universally compared to savage beasts by those who saw and felt their cruelty, and shuddered at the sight of the whole civilised world wasted by their lawless destructiveness. Yet these terrible savages, whom none could resist, were tamed and led by the Babe of Bethlehem, and became the founders of the kingdoms of Europe, and the strength of the Church of Christ.

Nor is the fulfilment historical only. Now is the time of the dominion of the Little Child. In our hearts He rules. What should we be, sinners and frail as we now are, what should we be, did not the " Little Child " lead and restrain us? What capacities for evil have we not within our bosom! The beast has one great instinct; in us there are the evil passions of many beasts. Do we not feel the murderous fury of the lion surging up sometimes within? Do we not notice the cunning stealthy creep of the leopard; the untiring following of revenge, like the pursuit of the wolf? Have we none of the venom of the serpent under our tongue; that member, as an Apostle says, more untameable than all beasts? Do we not know something of this, till we are positively afraid of ourselves? Who restrains, and governs, and leads us? Who but the "Little Child," the Babe of Bethlehem? Christ Himself specially taught that the spirit of a little child was the essence of His religion; to rule by meekness, to lead and govern and restrain and gain its ends, not by might or majesty, but by gentleness, by love. So it won its way in the world, so it conquers and holds possession of men now. This alone is the Spirit of the Gospel; no fear, no force, can make men Christians; they must be the willing captives of love, or live and die in lawless and lost freedom. They must be led by the "Little Child," or be the prey of the "Strong Man armed."

In the fold of Christ there is room for all sorts and conditions of men, the gentle lamb, the sportive kid, the peaceful calf, the useful cow, the patient and laborious ox; we can see what sort of people these indicate; and not these alone, but wolf and bear, leopard and lion; nay, even asp and cockatrice, these all may be taken in, tamed and led, and made happy and useful, by the gentle might of the "Little Child."

Let this then be our thought this Holy Innocents' Day. There is nothing too hard for the Lord. This world, so sinful, so lost, so out of harmony, may yet be restored; and these sinful, hardened souls about us may be brought into subjection; and these hard, untamed hearts within us, there is hope too for them, all through the power of the "Little Child," the Babe of Bethlehem.

Thursday after Christmas Day.

THE SIGN TO THE SHEPHERDS AND TO THE WORLD.

WHEN the angels appeared to the shepherds, they told them that they should find the new-born Saviour at Bethlehem, and that this should be "A sign unto them;" they should find the Babe "wrapped in swaddling clothes, lying in a manger." A sign to the shepherds, and a sign to all after ages. The world had looked and longed for a Saviour; men had yearned and prayed for a revelation of God, but no one had expected this. Men had trembled at the earthquake, the storm; they had gazed with bated breath at comets and signs in the heavens; when death had come suddenly, or pestilence had swept away its thousands, they said, "It is a visitation of God." There were legends of the gods coming in the likeness of men; but this visitation in great humility, this coming as a Babe, helpless, placing Himself at the mercy of His creatures, absolutely dependent for life and all things, this took the world by surprise; and the wonder has never ceased; no, nor never will.

The profound intelligences of the holy angels have never yet sounded the depths of this miracle of love. The saints have contemplated and meditated upon it, and still find it ever new, infinite, inexhaustible. The Old Testament Scriptures had foretold it, but it seemed too great for credence; and as time went on, and faith waxed cold, the great truth was explained away, and Israel expected nothing more than a deliverer from the Romans, another Moses, or another Maccabæus. They had lost the great hope of a Saviour of the world; God manifest; born of a Virgin; made very Man.

"This shall be a sign unto you;" God a little Babe; the Infinite circumscribed in that small frame; the Almighty weak, needing care; the Word of God dumb; the eternal Wisdom knowing nothing; "This shall be a sign unto you." What is the meaning of the sign? It is a revelation of God, a discovery of His character, never before known. Men knew something of the infinity of His greatness, but this displayed the infinity of His love. Men had never thought of self-sacrifice as an attribute of God; men had looked up with awe and fear; it was a new thing to look down upon a little wailing Babe, that claimed pity and protection, and learn something of God. In all ages men have searched for God; they have searched in height and depth, in the greatness of the mysteries of creation, in their own intellects, and the subtleties of reason and thought; but God has never revealed Himself in any of these; but only as a little Babe.

Oh, is there not a sign indeed here? Do we not see how God is to be found by finite creatures such as we, not by power and pride of intellect, but by humiliation and by purity? They who accept the sign, find God, a little Babe, a pure Virgin's child. The fall of angels and of men was through pride; man's restoration is by humility; and God Himself takes the first step, by humbling Himself.

"This shall be a sign unto you, ye shall find the Babe

wrapped in swaddling clothes." If the first sin of man is pride, the first and strongest instinct of the human heart is liberty; and therefore the Saviour of the world, who came to save man from himself and his lusts, having humbled Himself, next sacrificed His liberty. He lay bound hand and foot. Here again is the sign for all ages. To make us free, He gave up His liberty; to teach us true liberty, He revealed Himself bound. It was not the swaddling clothes, but the bands of love that held Him.

As He began, so He ended His life and its work. At Bethlehem He lay helpless, incapable of moving hand or foot; and upon the Cross it was the same; hands and feet were nailed fast, yet He was working; making us free. "This shall be a sign unto you." What is true liberty? It is subjection to law. God binds Himself by His own laws; the Son of God comes, and is obedient to parents, to rulers, to customs; above all, He subjects His will to the will and law of God, and bids us imitate His example. The cry of the unsanctified heart is "Liberty! No one shall interfere with me; I will do, and say, and think as I like; I am my own master; I will be free;" and the end is deepest and most degrading slavery; slavery to the passions; slavery to fashion and custom; slavery to evil ones; tied and bound now, tied and bound hereafter in outer darkness, where God is not. But they who see and accept this sign, become the bond slaves of Christ, and so are made free indeed; like Him slaves of love; most surely bound; most sweetly free; doing what they like best when doing His will; finding His yoke easy, His service perfect freedom.

"This shall be a sign unto you, ye shall find the Babe lying in a manger." Man by his sins has degraded himself to the level of the beasts; the Saviour who would lift man up, must place Himself below him. Man, who was but a little lower than the angels, is seen but little higher than the brute beasts; so God comes to find him there, and thence to raise him to his lost estate and yet higher. A sign this indeed of the infinite compassion of God; a sign of hope for the lowest fallen. Poor Prodigals and Magdalens have wandered far, have sounded the lowest depths of degradation, but God's pity has followed them even there. "If I go down to hell, Thou art there also." Among the beasts at His birth; between malefactors in His death; is not this a sign? Is not this good tidings of great joy to those who know the plague of their own hearts, and feel that it must be a far-reaching mercy that can avail for them?

"This shall be a sign unto you." "The ox knoweth his owner, and the ass his master's crib, but my people doth not consider." The animals are obedient to the law of their creation, and fulfil God's will; but man, made in the image of God, rebels to his own exceeding hurt. The telescope reveals God in infinite space, in immense creations, in inconceivable time; but the microscope reveals God in the infinitely little, and shows us, not ox and ass only doing His will, but tiniest creatures and lowest organisations. "Whither then can I go from Thy presence?" All creation is instinct with God; God is with us, though we know it not. Be this then our Christmas lesson to-day. Bethlehem is a revelation of God. He tells us something of what He is; how we may find Him; how we may become like Him. That we may enter into His Kingdom, we must be converted, and become as this little Child.

"This shall be a sign unto you." Let each take it home to himself. He who was content to lie in a manger will come and dwell with us if we will. Each Church is a Bethlehem, "The House of Bread," where the Bread of Life gives Himself in His wonderful Sacrament. The great King's birthday is kept; He bids us all to His feast, and says, "Ask what you will, and I will give it you;" let our answer be, "Lord, give me Thyself."

Friday after Christmas Day.

NO ROOM FOR GOD.

BETHLEHEM was but a small place; the influx caused by the taxing would fill the Inn; probably there was but one. Those who could pay best would be best served. Mary and Joseph were poor; they would travel on foot and slowly, and so come late. We can well understand then that they would find all places occupied, and no room for them. Even now-a-days, when travelling is made so easy, there is scarcely anything that brings out petty selfishness more; the rule seems to be, every one for himself, and let the weaker go to the wall. The sweet, lowly Mary was not one to push and protest; her condition might command gentle consideration, but men did not notice, and only pushed by, eager after food; and even women, who would notice what men did not see, were not self-denying enough to give up their comfort for their sister in her time of need. No one befriended Mary; and so she crept away to the dark recesses of the cave that served for the stable of the Inn, and there alone, in silence, in darkness; exempted she alone from Eve's curse; she clasped in her arms her Child and her God, and joy unspeakable reigned in her heart.

It is all full of mystery, beauty, and wonder; we too would fain get away to that quiet dim place, and with Mary adore in wrapt silence, and ponder in our hearts, too full to speak. There are volumes upon volumes of holy lore revealed in that little Babe; what He is; what He does; what He has chosen, what rejected; who are His companions, who know and acknowledge Him, and who are ignorant of Him; what the world is to Him, and He to the world. Time would fail even to catalogue the topics of thought and meditation; eternity will not be too long to pore over them, and search out their sweetness and satisfying delights.

But turn we to one thought, homely, grave, most pregnant and instructive, convenient for us in this our state of probation, appropriate for this Christmas season. "There was no room for them in the Inn." The way of the world! A poet of our own, rich, noble, a man of the world, has left it on record how he had often "Found his warmest welcome at an Inn;" a welcome bought with money; a welcome he found not in any home of his own, for selfishness and profligacy had made him homeless; but money and rank and fame made him welcome in some places. The way of the world!

Is not the world itself like an Inn? Men come and go; they are as guests that tarry but a day; and those who can pay for it, get the world's best. There are others, skilled in little arts of selfishness, who manage to slip into good places, and secure comforts and attention. A little self-assertion, a little pushing and contriving, a little flattery and soft speaking, or a little overbearing insolence, as occasion demands; who that has travelled knows not the place and the reward of these things? Who does not see in all a picture of the way of the world in the daily routine of the Inn?

"There was no room for them in the Inn;" for Joseph and Mary and Jesus. Oh most true prophecy for all time;

a simple, pure man and woman, gentle, most holy, without money or rank; what room for such, where human nature is pushing on, and selfishness is the rule? God made Man, a weak Babe, dependent upon loving, wise, divinely-taught intuition, what room for Him? The world is lauding and obeying Cæsar, who has climbed to power by force, who has waded to the purple through blood, and who rules now by might and terror, and lives a life of profligacy and self-indulgence. Yes, this is the master the world will bow down to. The world is busy with plans and schemes; it is in a hurry; it has its own affairs to attend to; there is no room for God. So the Roman world decided when God came and His Kingdom began to be set up. At first it was too busy to notice the intrusion, and simply ignored it, and thrust it aside. But presently the Kingdom grew and spread, and became inconvenient; then said the world, "This will not do; I must be master here; there is not room for two; submit, or I will crush you." Then came a reign of terror for three hundred years; and its watchword was this, "There is no room for you here." Persecution raged, and the world tried to stamp out Christianity; but in the caves of the earth, as at Bethlehem, there was found shelter, till the tyranny was overpast. Then came the day long prophesied, when the kingdoms of the world became the Kingdom of God and His Christ. But still the world's heart was not converted. There was outward subjection, but inward corruption. The world corrupted what it could not destroy, and then turned round in well simulated, virtuous indignation, and demanded the destruction of what was a sham and a lie.

In our own day the cry is ever rising deep and loud against the Kingdom of Christ, "There is no room for

Thee; we want all men's energies for this world and its schemes; money and time and labour, we cannot spare them for God, we want them all for ourselves. This life is a certainty, the life to come may perhaps be a myth; man and his wants are realities, God and His demands may wait; perhaps there is no God. If there must be religion, let it keep its place; let it get out of our way; we can get on very well without it. Take it away to the stable, if you like; we will not have it here in the Inn; there is no room for it, we want every inch for eating and drinking, for talking and transacting our business." So cries the world. Religion is separated from government; the State sets aside the name of God, and rules in its own name. If differences arise, the State must have its way, and religion must be made to submit. God is excluded from senate and school, from public measures and business life; Herod's sword is not just yet drawn, but God is sent away to the dark cave with the dumb beasts.

But let us come nearer home. God comes not to the world only, but to each human heart; and each human heart is a world in miniature. How many a heart is like the world, because it is like an Inn. Compare an Inn with a private house, and notice the points of difference and contrast. The one, the home of one family, the other the common resort of any who cares to lodge there, and pay for it. We English especially know what home is, and glory in it; we have proverbs and popular songs that embody the national convictions that "An Englishman's house is his castle," and that, "Be it never so homely, there's no place like home." Some hearts are like a pure, happy English home, and some are like an Inn; like that Inn at Bethlehem, where there was no room for God. There is always room in a home for a member of the family, always a welcome, even for an unexpected arrival. An Inn has no small power of expansion in its accommodation, if the comer has money to spend; but the poor are not welcome when the house is full. Are not many hearts like this? The open door lets in all comers, there is no sense of privacy or repose; there are loud voices, excited faces, hurry, everlasting change. In that corner drunkenness, in another lust, in another fraud; no one knows his neighbour; names are dropped, and numbers substituted; day is turned into night, and night into day; Sunday is the same as week days. Is there not something like this in many a heart? It is full; it is restless; it has guests of all kinds, and often changing; dark deeds are done; schemes are hatched; unhallowed persons come and go unchallenged; new faces are welcomed; only there is no room for God; no time for prayer or worship; no money for alms, no inclination for Christ-like acts of mercy and charity. The life is filled up, and no place has been left for God. That man is striving hard at his business, his heart is full of it; there is no room for God. That woman lives for her children and house, and has no room for God. Some lounge through life, and have nothing to do, and yet they do not find room for God, even in their thoughts. The rich man in the parable fared sumptuously every day, and was clothed in purple and fine linen, while Lazarus lay at his gate with the dogs. The men in the Inn at Bethlehem made themselves as comfortable as they could, while God lodged in the stable with their horses. We may make excuse for them, and say, they did not know it. But is it not always so with the visits of God? Our Lord Himself tells us that this will be the standing defence at the

NO ROOM FOR GOD.

last day, "When saw we Thee, and treated Thee so?" And He says that He will not accept the excuse.

Many stay away from Communion; one has one excuse, another another. Is not the real reason with all, that they have no room for God? Advent has been the time for making ready; Zacchæus has heard, and heeded, he has made haste, and made ready, and he receives his Lord joyfully, and makes amends for past faults. Martha and Mary have heard, and their home at Bethany is all bright, ready to welcome the weary, rejected Jesus. Children come home; friends arrive; families are gathered; but in some homes, and in some hearts, there is no room for God. He is not expected, He is not invited, He is not wanted. If he comes He will have to lodge with the beasts. "The ox knoweth his owner, the ass his master's crib." The beasts fulfil their vocation, and rebel not against their Maker, but men and women, made in the image of God, can live without Him in disobedience, and yet care not, fear not. What is Christmas to us? Christmas with God, or Christmas without God? "God with us," or, "No room for Him?" Will He come to such as we are? Ay, He will now, as before, be guest with a man that is a sinner; provided always the sinner be penitent. He who came again and again to the cottage at Bethany; He who dwelt in the lowly Home at Nazareth, He will not refuse to come to any who has prepared Him a lodging. He who as at this time, for love of us and for our salvation, laid aside His eternal and awful majesty, and stooped so very low, that he might touch the very lowest depths of humiliation, will not despise one heart that opens itself to Him, but will be to him "Jesus," and save him from his sins.

New Year's Eve.

THE END OF THE WORLD.

WHEN St. Peter's words, "The end of all things is at hand," are read in these days, people say, "Ah, you see St. Peter was mistaken, just as St. Paul was mistaken in the same matter; they both imagined that Christ would return to judgment during their life-time. The same mistake has been made many times since. There was a general belief that the year 1000 after Christ would bring the end of the world; people gave themselves up to its expectation, left the land untilled, neglected business and the duties of life, and wandered about, waiting and listening for the sounding of the last trump. Before that, when the hordes of wild savages from the north poured in upon the Roman Empire, and pillaged and burned and destroyed, and reduced beautiful and populous cities to silent ruinous solitudes, men confidently declared that the times of the end had come, and that the prophesied signs were evident and unmistakeable. Books have been written and preachers have fulminated the same thing over and over again; a comet, an earthquake, a war, a pestilence, a new reading of the Bible, a new calculation of dates, or another interpretation of some particular sign of Antichrist, has been made the occasion of an alarm about the end of the world, and has frightened a few silly people. But we are wiser than to be taken in by this sort of nonsense ; the world will go on, as it has gone on, in spite of such dreams and scares ; sensible people can afford to smile at alarmists and fanatics, and to feel certain that nature will follow its unalterable laws, and pursue an unswerving course, as it has ever done. The last conclusions of science are opposed to the theory of catastrophes, and account for all phenomena by infinitely slow processes spread over vast periods of time."

Such is the way in which people now-a-days treat the idea of "The end of the world," and the prophecies of our Lord and His Apostles of the burning up of all things by a judgment of fire. And yet even the most recent discoveries of science make such a catastrophe by no means impossible. Thus we are told, "The Comet of 1843, whose tail stretched half-way across the sky, must actually have grazed the Sun's surface, while its nucleus was more than 160,000 miles in diameter. There may be much vaster comets, whose orbits may intersect the Sun's surface, followed by flights of meteoric masses, enormous in size and many in number, which falling upon the Sun with the enormous velocity of some 360 miles in a second, would excite his whole frame to a degree of heat far exceeding what he now emits. In 1859 an intensely bright spot was seen on the Sun's surface, supposed to be the result of the impact of some huge meteoric masses. Though the outburst lasted but a few minutes, the whole frame of the earth was sensibly affected; vivid auroras were seen in both hemispheres, and where they are seldom seen; electric disturbance took place, telegraphs became useless, the clerks receiving sharp shocks ; in some places fire broke out. We can therefore conceive that a very large comet, followed by a dense mass of meteors falling upon the Sun's surface for a few days, would so excite the Sun's heat that every living thing upon the earth would inevitably be destroyed."

Nor is this a possibility only. More than once astronomers have seen small stars suddenly increase enormously in brightness, and by Spectrum-analysis have found them to be suns like our own, but by some unknown means urged into such a condition of furious heat, that if they have planets like those of our system, those planets must have been inevitably destroyed. It is urged, that among the millions of suns and systems which our telescopes reveal to us, such catastrophes are so rare that the chances against the destruction of any one system by such an event are enormously great, and need not be entertained. But it may be replied, that Scripture foretells the end of the world by fire, and science shows how it may very well happen according to natural laws and experience; and if it is God's will that the end shall come in this way, doubtless the means are prepared, and in spite of the law of chances they will most surely do their work at the appointed time. Man's imperfect knowledge of the laws of the universe made St. Peter's words seem unlikely to be realised when they were written; our increased knowledge, instead of making them still more improbable, now shows their physical possibility. "The heavens shall pass away with a great noise, and the elements shall melt with fervent heat, the earth also and the works that are therein shall be burned up."

Nor is this all; the latest discoveries of science tell us that if such a catastrophe happened, it might come in a moment, without the slightest warning. During the last eclipse of the sun, a bright comet was discovered close to its surface, of which the astronomers had no knowledge before. It had come they knew not when, or whence.

The warning therefore of "The end of all things" is never out of date. It was true in St. Peter's days that it was "at hand," and it is true now, and will be till the event itself comes; for "Of that day and hour knoweth no man." It will come "As a thief in the night, and when men say, peace and safety, then sudden destruction cometh." Let it be understood, however, that we do not say that the end of the world *will* come in this way, but only that modern physical science in its most mature conclusions shows that it *may* so come, and that here at least the Bible and science are entirely agreed.

Such thoughts seem fitting for us on such a day as this, when we are at the end of another year. The end of the year may well make us think of "The end of all things;" not to rouse morbid feelings, or to excite fanaticism, but to remind us of the inspired assurance that this world will come to an end with all that is in it; and so to teach us the true value of all earthly things as compared with those things that cannot be destroyed, either by fire, or lapse of time, or aught else. For surely we need not look on to the end of the world to feel the truth of the assurance that "All things come to an end." Things come to an end before our eyes; change and death are everywhere at work. Let us look back at the past year, each from his own standpoint; what changes have come! how many deaths have carried off those who were this time last year as we are now. Death is "at hand" for each one of us. It is not merely increasing years that bring death nearer to us, but it is the uncertainty of its approach; the thousand ways, by accident, or by sickness, by which it may suddenly and by speedy and short process, lay us in our graves. Death is a terrible, inevitable necessity. It thrusts itself among the possibilities of every year, nay, of every day. It is just like the end of the world in this, that while it seems unlikely to happen just now, there is no one that can say it will not happen immediately. There is no time when it may not be said to be "at hand." Death is also in another way like the end of the world, that it is for each "The end of all things." Marriage is by God's law indissoluble; but even in marriage there is the promise, "Till death us do part;" death ends the relationship. So with appointments of trust; so with property and possessions; death ends all; the dead hand cannot hold these things, however precious and hard-earned they may have been; "We can take nothing out of the world." We all have plans and hopes, we look forward, we prepare for the future, but death may step in, uninvited, unexpected, most inconveniently, and spoil all, end all. We see it happening constantly; it may happen to us. Age and health may be supposed to have something to do with probabilities, but we cannot be certain of anything, only that death will certainly come, and that we know not when it may come.

A great part of men's sins and carelessness come through neglect of this, forgetfulness of it, getting into a dull stolid animal way of living only in the present moment. "Because sentence against an evil work is not speedily executed, the hearts of the children of men are wholly set in them to do evil." Men sin, and are not punished at once; they do wrong and neglect duty, and are none the worse for it, and so they take courage, and get into the habit of living as they like, just as it happens, and think it will go on for ever. Or rather they do not think at all, and presently lose the power of thinking about it, and get fixed and hardened, till nothing can rouse them, nothing bring them to repentance. There are many living in this way before our eyes, without prayer, or worship, or sacraments; eating, sleeping, working, taking their pleasure, without any fear, any anxiety, any thought of heaven and hell; mere higher animals, living without reference to God or responsibility to Him, or thought of the end, and of the Judgment beyond. Among those who come to Church many display this same hardening of the conscience; they say penitential words as if they were reading a newspaper; they hear sermons, and it never seems to strike them to apply what they hear to themselves; they keep away from Holy Communion, or come merely because they have a custom to do so, without a particle of feeling, or a sign of amendment of life. Now the end of all this is at hand. It cannot go on for ever. It will not go on much longer. There will be a rude and rough awakening presently, and some very terrible experiences.

But there is another way of thinking of "The end of all things," and that is, as we think of the harvest as the end of the year's work. Everything we do works results. It has been said truly, "The boy is the father of the man;" so this year is what it is because of last year, and the years before it. We are what we are to-day through what we have been and have done in days and years gone by; and the end is coming that will seal up and fix all things. Just as the sculptor works days and weeks, and at the end there is a figure, the result of all his work, so are we day by day, and year by year, making our souls into some definite shape, the result of deeds and thoughts, that may seem little in themselves, but each of which leaves its mark and influence upon us.

Oh those terrible words, "The end of those things is death." What do they mean? We know not; only we are sure it must be something most dreadful to reasonable, spiritual beings. Death that affects the body is terrible to human nature; death that is but for a moment; but what must be "Eternal Death;" death that attacks the soul with its exquisite sensibilities, its aspirations? "O Lord God most holy, O Lord most mighty, O holy and most merciful Saviour, deliver us not into the bitter pains of eternal death."

We sometimes hear weak and stupid people say, "I wish I were dead." They are in pain, or sickness, or trouble, and they lazily and impatiently want to be relieved; and so they profess to wish for death as the end of what they suffer. But death is not only an end but a beginning. The end of Winter is Spring; the end of Boyhood is Manhood; so the end of Time is Eternity. After death there is the life of the world to come. This is what makes death so solemn, so tremendous; that great awful unknown future, that life that ends not, where there is no repentance, no opportunity to correct mistakes, to make up for time lost, to undo evil doings, to build up the soul in likeness to Christ, to prepare to meet God, and to be fit to dwell with Him.

"The end of all things is at hand." There are many to whom these words give quiet consolation. How often do we say, "Thank God, that is over!" What a sense of relief when a suffering, an anxiety is finished, a desired end attained, a difficulty overcome. Children, some few persons temporarily intoxicated with a gratification, stupid animal beings who have dull sensibilities and no high aspirations, may be satisfied with this life and with the world; but thoughtful men and women, who have weighed the good and evil of human life, who have appraised their own prospects and chances of happiness, not in moments of pleasure, nor in dull hours of agony or bitter disappointment, not by their own experience only, but by the verdict of ages, the testimony not only of this wise person and that, but by the united voice of that which represents the wisdom of mankind, have said with Job, "I would not live alway." They have no hope of the curing of the world's ills; they have earnest thoughts, high hopes, grand ideals, which all seem possible, all appear man's rightful inheritance, but they despair of seeing the realisation for the world and for themselves of these bright visions. They groan at the sight of the abuses, the miseries, the futile attempts at reform, the failures, the waste of the best things, the blindness, the madness, the stupidity of mankind; and the thought that all this will not go on for ever is a deep, quiet satisfaction to them. The assured conviction that death will cure all that nothing else can cure casts a bright warm tint upon their souls, like the glance of the setting sun from among dark clouds at the end of a dull, cheerless day.

Nor is this all; we believe not only in the end of this world's evil, but in the coming of a better life. St. John tells us, "I saw a new heaven and a new earth, for the first heaven and the first earth were passed away; and I heard a great voice out of heaven, saying, God shall wipe away all tears, and there shall be no more death, neither sorrow nor crying, neither shall there be any more pain." Shall we give up this hope? Human life is such a puzzle to the thoughtful man, that it seems at last as if we understood it as little as the animals understand us and our ways with them; and the end must be blank fatalism or despairing atheism, unless we accept Christ's prescription, and take life upon trust, as the little loving trustful child takes his father's doings upon trust, and loves and hopes and clings to him, even in pain and tears and fear. Clever men, who have reasoned themselves into blind denial of God, are trying to frame a system of morals and of reasonable religion with the supernatural left out, without a future life, without rewards and punishments after death; but they evidently and hopelessly fail, and must fail. We cannot be mere animals, for our souls will not be crushed and silenced. We cannot go back to the old heathenism; it did not satisfy the wise and the great in its own day, how can it possibly be all we want in these last days of the manhood of mankind? It must be Christ, or no one; Christ or nothing; Christ who is Light, or darkness that will be felt in chilling, paralysing, deadening chaos, overwhelming the magnificent soul of man.

Oh let us draw nearer to Christ, cling closer to Christ, trust in Him entirely, believe in Him more and more unreservedly. He is the one hope of humanity; the one cure for the world's ill and of the sorrows of mankind. And better still, He is the one and only Friend and Saviour of individual souls; the one firm immoveable rest amidst the shifting, changing, passing, disappointing lapse of all things. He is the Rock amidst the sand; He is "I am," with whom is no past, no future; He is Alpha and Omega, beginning and end, first and last. With His Name let us end this year; with His newly assumed name Jesus, let us begin a new year; with Him let us spend each day. Let His Name be the last utterance of our dying lips, the last sound that enters our ears, ere they close to all earthly sounds. May his dear Face meet our first bewildered gaze upon another world; may His dear Hand meet ours as we feel about in the darkness where no human hand can lead us; may we find Him "The End of all things," the solution of all riddles, the satisfaction of all hopes, the harbour of refuge of our tempest-tossed souls, our Saviour, our Lord, our all.

New Year's Day.

CHRIST'S FIRST TASTE OF HUMAN SORROW.

For seven days deep ineffable peace, and joy that was altogether of heaven, brooded over and possessed the souls of the Holy Family at Bethlehem. But it could last no longer. He who could not rest in heaven till man was saved, could not rest beyond the seventh day without uniting Himself with man yet more intimately by the all-potent sympathy of suffering. On the eighth day "The Babe wept," wept under the sense of sharp pain; wept tears that were prophetic of Bethany and Olivet; shed Blood that told of Gethsemane and of Calvary. Heaven was indeed joined to earth when God became man, when the Son of God was seen as a Babe; but the union was proved beyond all question when God felt human sorrow.

Christmas is supernatural light in the time of darkness; but the Circumcision is that first lurid red streak of morning light that tells of rain and storm the whole coming day. Well then does this commemoration stand at the beginning of the year, for "Man is born to trouble." "Sorrow is the very substance of man's natural life. The power of art is in the sorrowful; no poetry, no music, ever penetrates and dwells in the mind like that which has in it a burden of sorrow. Sorrow is the very poetry of a creation which is fallen; of a race which is in exile. Sympathy is the bond of hearts, and all sympathy has some of the blood of sorrow in its veins." It is believed that the sinless Body of Christ was not subject to disease; but that He might feel our infirmity He suffered pain, and that as soon as might be. And so it was ordained that the Holy One should be nameless till He had begun to know human pain and sorrow. When first His Blood was shed; when tears wrung forth by pain first filled His eyes, then He was called Jesus. Jesus the Saviour of men. "Strange thought, that there were seven days during which our Blessed Lord was nameless! He who was the Word of God, whose mouth spake and it was done, who commanded and Creation came forth; He was a speechless, nameless Infant! Oh ineffable mystery! Oh immense love! But with the shedding of His Blood comes the blessed name of Jesus; as if He had no right to it until He had shed His Blood. And now evermore this commemoration braids upon the front of every coming year of life the Name of Jesus; braids it in those red drops of His Infancy, the first blossoms of His Precious Blood."

Circumcision then, cruel as it seemed, was nevertheless responsive to the voice of nature, for even infancy suffers, and nothing is more moving than the sad cry of pain that is wrung from a suffering child. And we, who are to become as little children, we must be circumcised with Christ, mortified, trained, restrained, as children must be, until we come to the fulness of the stature of Christ, stretched with Him upon the Cross, that so with Him we may rise and reign.

"Behold the Babe wept;" He who made the world, and even then was upholding all things by the word of

His power, He wept upon the bosom of His Mother. Here is a thought for us to meditate upon to-day, down upon our knees, wrapt in heavenly contemplation. Here is that which tells us more of God, and of Christ, and of their love, and of our wisdom and duty, than all learning, all books, all sermons. "Behold the Babe wept;" the same who presently should say, "Blessed are they that mourn, for they shall be comforted."

Is Christ's religion then a thing of tears and sadness, repulsive, gloomy, unnatural? God forbid; the truth is this, man's life, as all know by their own experience, is deeply tinted with sadness; tears are ever seen at all the chief events of life; at birth, at marriage, at death; and we never think them out of place at any of those events. There is indeed a land where all tears shall be wiped away, but it is not here. Here the most loving thing God could do for us was to come into the world and weep with those that wept. He might not take away the thorns that sprang up from the cursed ground, but this He did, He bound them round His own Head, that their sharp points might be sheathed there, instead of in our hearts. There are still thorns, but He has made them to bear roses; there are still tears, but He has taken away their bitterness, and shed a balmy blessedness over His own who mourn, Himself their Comforter.

We may ask why this is? Why He who could do all things, could not have now wiped away all tears, and spared those whom He loves their many sorrows. But we can get no answer to our question; only we see that He who could have saved us otherwise, saved us by that way which cost Himself most. If then He wills that we suffer awhile, we remember that He also suffered. If He will have us live our life out, before He gives us rest and bliss, we know how He lived His thirty-three years patiently, with the Cross ever in view. We remember how He allowed Lazarus to die, when He might have healed him, and Martha and Mary to weep and suffer, when a word would have saved them; how He left His loved Apostles in the world, to work, to suffer, to be martyred, and would not pray His Father to take them out of the world, but only to keep them from the evil. This then is His way. It is no new thing that befalls us, "Jesus Christ is the same yesterday, to-day, and for ever." Human life under Christianity is still human life; the godly man suffers like the wicked. Solomon could not understand this, but One greater than Solomon has made it plain to us. David was grieved at this, but David's Son has cast in His lot with us, to show that the Son is chastened not in anger, but in loving discipline that is needful, and worketh perfection.

Let us then this New Year's Day take our prospective view of the coming year through the medium of the atmosphere of this day's commemoration. The flatterers, who are but mockers cunningly and gaily disguised, will tell us that all will be well with us this year, and bid us be happy without limit or end; like the old courtly phrasing that bade the king "live for ever." But our hearts cannot rise to the thought; we know it is not true; that it cannot be. Then others will come with woful countenance and sighs, and groan out congratulations that covertly imply that there is nothing before us but suffering and misery; as if the perfection of religion were to make us dismal, and to add new horrors to the catalogue of evils that are ours by nature already. Let all these maskers stand aside; let the unveiled face of honest truth greet us to-day; let us set out on our New Year with the

Babe at Bethlehem. We know then the worst and best; neither joy nor sorrow can take us unawares. The Babe weeps to-day, but He promises and gives blessing therefore to all who weep. There is the dark future of Calvary, but Easter-day's light shines brightly beyond. There is the pilgrimage of thirty-three years, but there is the Home with him afterwards. The coming year will not, we know, be all joy, but neither will it be all sorrow. There will come changes, some for better, some for worse, but Jesus changes not; He is the same yesterday, to-day, for ever; if He be with us, we need fear no evil, for all things will work for good.

On the eighth day, the day of Circumcision, the Babe weeps. On the eighth day, the day of Resurrection, the Lord of life rejoices. The great eighth day comes for us, the day of plenary circumcision, the putting off, not part, but the whole flesh, in which is sin and death; the entering into the presence of God in His Temple, of which the admission of the new-born child to the Temple at Jerusalem was the type. We are embarked upon the great ocean of life, and all is change, all is restless motion around us; sea and ship, mast and sails, all are in uneasy motion, but the haven, where we would be, that stands firm and steady; there alone is rest. In the day, the white sheltering cliffs that break the force of wind and sea, and make a great calm within, and at night the bright beacon-light, steady and clear, that we may go by day and by night. We change with the changing years, but He changes not; His Name is Jesus, always Jesus, Jesus the Saviour, "God with us." His Name is wonderful, for it can do all things; it is above every name; by it diseases were healed, the blind were made to see, the lame to walk, the dead to live. That Name has been the hope of all

Christian souls in every year since it was preached to the world; let it be our hope this New Year every day. "Think how many of God's servants have gone out of the world with this most sweet Name on their lips and in their hearts; think how many death-beds have heard that Name as the last of all earthly sounds; how many martyrs have uttered it just before they received the death stroke; how often in storms at sea, just as the ship went down; in battles, in terrors, in dangers, God's servants have found time to call upon that adorable Name, and have been heard, and helped." "The Name of the Lord is a strong tower, the righteous runneth into it, and is safe."

In the Name of the Lord then let us enter upon this New Year; so every sorrow that comes upon us will be cheered and sweetened by the presence and comfort of Him Whose Name is ever Jesus; upon Whom we wholly rest; in Whom we wholly trust; and to Whom, with the Father and the Holy Ghost, be ascribed this day and every day, all honour and glory, might, majesty, and dominion. Amen.

By the same Author.

A MANUAL FOR LENT.

MEDITATIONS FOR EVERY DAY, AND FOR THE SUNDAYS AND EASTER-TIDE.

Second Edition. 3s. 6d.

"A thoughtful book."—*Church Bells.*

"Will be useful to those who desire to add to their private devotions at this Season some spiritual reading that will afford matter for meditation and prayer."—*Church Times.*

"The difficulty experienced by many in finding suitable recreation during the Lenten season is well known in many households; for whilst light frivolous reading is scarcely admissible, some variety from strictly formal devotional literature is essential to keep the mind in a healthy condition. This is provided in the Rev. F. C. Woodhouse's Manual. The Author has been careful to make each discourse appropriate for the day on which it is to be read, and suggestive of thoughts calculated to advance the spiritual welfare of the reader. Many of the discourses are particularly attractive; amongst which may be mentioned those on the 'Education of the Conscience,' 'Safeguards for the great Middle Class of Christians,' and on 'Spiritual Manhood;' although these are by no means the only ones worthy of meditation. The style as well as the subjects selected, which are from both Old and New Testaments, will please a large number of readers."—*Public Opinion.*

"Very seasonable and full of matter for earnest meditation is 'A Manual for Lent.' Rev. F. C. Woodhouse is no mere stringer together of common-places. The chapter on the 'Difficulty of Easter Joy' has a freshness seldom found in books of this kind, and that on Easter Eve is peculiarly suggestive, at a time when Bishop Magee, in the recent correspondence about Prayers for the Dead, has been turning men's thoughts to the condition of the Faithful Departed. We heartily recommend the book as among the best of those put forth by a Firm which has already gained a high position among Church publishers."—*Graphic.*

THE LIFE OF THE SOUL IN THE WORLD;

ITS NATURE, NEEDS, DANGERS, SORROWS, AIDS, AND JOYS. 3s. 6d.

"It is written in an earnest, loving spirit. It is free from useless verbiage, and is intensely real."—*National Church.*

"A really valuable contribution to our too scanty books of devotion, with a true English ring in it. Suited for a gift book in times of sorrow."—*John Bull.*

"There are few better books for educated Christians."—*Church Bells.*

"There is something new in the method of thought pursued by the writer of this work. It is suited to help the Christian to develop the devotional faculty of his soul. There is nothing dull, uninteresting, or unprofitable in the whole book. Some parts remind us of Bunyan's Allegory, inasmuch as it partakes of the same serenity and inspiration."—*Christian Union.*

"A book of great merit, connecting morals in practical life and the devotion of the heart, with the means of grace in this life, and future hope of the next. It is written in excellent style, with ample reference and allusions to modern authors of experience, and would be exactly the book to put in the way of men whom sickness or trouble has stirred to enquire into the theory and practice of religion. Manly books are much needed, and this seems thoroughly to deserve such a description."—*Guardian.*

"Every chapter will reveal not only the hidden difficulties and dangers incident to spiritual life, but the only effectual remedy against them."—*Christian Opinion.*

"Fervent without asceticism, and admirably adapted for private edification."—*American Literary Churchman.*

"Much to be recommended to the thoughtful, and commended for its plain outspokenness."—*Morning Post.*

"Helpful in the work of sanctification."—*Nonconformist.*

"Much that is deserving of commendation."—*Record.*

"No one can read it without feeling that he is a more learned, if not a wiser man. We would strongly recommend to our younger clergy the reading of this book. It gives a vast amount of matter required by them in their everyday labours in a thoroughly condensed and pure English style. They may easily extend the articles, but it would be no trifling labour to condense them."—*Ecclesiastical Gazette.*

"Earnest in tone, and we do not doubt they will be found helpful. Remarkably copious quotations from the literature of the day."—*School Guardian.*

"A very edifying course of spiritual reading."—*Church Times.*

"Much to be recommended to the busy men in the world, and to the overworked preacher. There is throughout a loyal devotion to the Church."—*Church Review.*

"A book which we can most heartily and conscientiously recommend."—*Clerical World.*

THE MILITARY RELIGIOUS ORDERS OF THE MIDDLE AGES.

THE HOSPITALLERS, THE TEMPLARS, THE TEUTONIC KNIGHTS, AND OTHERS,

WITH AN APPENDIX OF OTHER ORDERS OF KNIGHTHOOD, LEGENDARY, HONORARY, AND MODERN. 3*s*. 6*d*.

"The book presents a great deal of out-of-the-way information in a readable form."—*Scotsman.*

"A unique study, in which will be found not merely exceedingly well-arranged historical facts, but often very judicious estimates of the force and value of the singular movements of which these Orders were the leaders."—*Nonconformist.*

"Will be read with pleasure. There is much historic information."—*Church Review.*

"A work of singular interest."—*Church Times.*

"The ever-interesting story is told well."—*Guardian.*

"A very mine of information on a subject which is comparatively unknown."—*English Churchman.*

"Instructive and interesting."—*Aberdeen Free Press.*

SPIRITUAL LESSONS TAUGHT BY DUMB ANIMALS. 1s.

"Extremely well done. Not at all dry."—*School Guardian.*

"An excellent little volume."—*Church Times.*

"A capital chapter in Natural History."—*Irish Ecclesiastical Gazette.*

"It might be thought that there was very little that was new to be said on such subjects, but that would be a mistake."—*Church Bells.*

THE EXEMPLAR OF PENITENCE:
MEDITATIONS ON THE FIFTY-FIRST PSALM. 1s. 6d.

"Thoroughly well-conceived, and full of suggestive thought."—*Literary Churchman.*

"Short, pithy, and effective. There is no lack of wholesome, vigorous, and thoroughly devotional material."—*Church Times.*

"Very useful for Lent."—*Church Review.*

"Short but effective."—*Church Herald.*

www.ingramcontent.com/pod-product-compliance
Lightning Source LLC
Chambersburg PA
CBHW020756230426
43666CB00007B/720